About the Author

How does one sift the wheat from the chaff? I started by reading some of my old diaries and poems – and I did a lot of painful soul-searching. I can't say I've had a bad life; it could have been better, but then that is true for us all. I'm sure we could all benefit from an analyst, a life-style coach and a personal trainer. However, my intention was not to complain about my life, but to examine it with a view to gathering some understanding. For, like Horace Walpole, I do not understand anything until I have written it down. At various times in my life I have tried to improve myself by reading such subjects as philosophy, psychology, sociology and science. I am by no means an expert on any of these subjects, I just have an enquiring mind. This is essentially a coming of age saga, with a lot of bad poetry, some regret and I hope, a modicum growth.

An Ordinary Life Revisited

Peter John Dorrell

An Ordinary Life Revisited

Olympia Publishers
London

www.olympiapublishers.com
OLYMPIA PAPERBACK EDITION

A CIP catalogue record for this title is
available from the British Library.

ISBN: 978-1-78830-481-8

First Published in 2020

Olympia Publishers
Tallis House
2 Tallis Street
London
EC4Y 0AB

Printed in Great Britain

Wistful

The knights of old were big and bold
But I am only weak
The knights would go to war and fight
But I play hide-and-seek

I wish I had a shiny sword
And rode upon a horse
But now my mother has arrived
With pie and chocolate sauce

One

This is the story of my life; it has been a very unexceptional life and my only excuse for having written it, is that on my retirement I had an irresistible urge to understand my life — what had it all been about? I dare say I'm no exception in failing to fully appreciate my life at the time it was being lived, for as Soren Kierkegaard said: "Life can only be understood backwards, but must be lived forwards."

But be warned. There are many reasons for not reading this book: it is probably badly written, no doubt contains a lot of boring autobiography, and tells no coherent story. It is full of bad poetry, trivial musings, superficial rants and facile observations. Much of it sounds didactic, but at the time of writing I was merely trying to clarify my own thinking. My only excuse for having completed this book is that once started, I couldn't stop.

I started this book soon after having enrolled for a creative writing course at my local college. Enrolling for the course was an impulsive decision: I looked through the prospectus, felt I should do *something,* and "Creative Writing" seemed the most appealing. I had fancied being a writer in my youth, but this had even less reality than children wanting to be train drivers, and for various reasons I left school barely able to write.

At the college Mr Miller encouraged us to write from the heart about our own experiences. He suggested we might start with a school recollection. I wrote about an incident that happened at my primary school:

A Minor Protest in the Classroom

I would like to describe an incident that occurred at my primary school in 1944. I had just returned to school after a period of illness — nothing serious, just one of the common complaints that children got in those days, and I took my usual seat at the back of the class.

On being given an arithmetic book and an appropriate page number, everybody started scribbling away, everybody, that is, except me. I couldn't understand this new arithmetic — "long division" — nor did I find the teacher's example on the blackboard of any help. I couldn't see her figures — I was soon to discover that I needed glasses.

As a consequence, I was "demoted" from the first to the fourth stream. The fourth stream was full of girls, and not then having reached puberty, I was not happy, in fact, I was deeply humiliated. I felt the whole class was laughing at my expense.

At the start of the next maths class, we were again given an arithmetic book and told to do as many sums as we could, I considered the simple sums of adding, subtraction, multiplication, and division far too easy, and allowing no time to double check my figure, I tore through one section after another.

At the end of the allotted time, we were told to swap our books with the person in front, the teacher then proceeded to read out the answers. After a while, the teacher asked if any books had still to be marked — a few still had. A short time later, however, only the girl marking my exercise book was raising her hand.

More answers were read out, and the teacher asked the same question. "My girl" shot her hand up again, "I've a lot more yet, miss." By now, the whole class was taking an interest, and every time the hand shot up the class began to titter, and I hugged myself in anticipation. At the end of the lesson the teacher gave me a quizzical look, beckoned me from my seat, and then pointed to my old place in the first stream. It was good, once more, to be where I felt I belonged.

Mr Miller assumed this incident might have been a "pivotal one", that it might have led to self-awareness, self-confidence and academic success. I wished I could have affirmed this. The truth was, it made no difference — I was not a bright child, I saw learning as a chore, my only inclination was to have fun with my mates.

We were then asked to write about our earliest recollections. What was my earliest? I remember riding my tiny tricycle down a hill, and on becoming scared that I was travelling too fast, I stretched out my hand and ran it along a tall garden fence, hoping to reduce my speed; as a consequence, I toppled over, hurt my knee and cried.

When I mentioned this story to my mother, she told me that a young girl, who at the time lived next door, sat me down beside her and carefully removed from my hand the splinters from the fence — I then recalled the young girl doing this. My mother told me that during the short time we lived at that address, this girl had thought the world of me, and would look after me.

Was *that* a pivotal experience? I cannot recall any affection from within my home; I cannot recall kissing, or being kissed, by my mother, and a hug from Dad would have been out of the question. Not that I would have welcomed such attention, quite the contrary, for I can still recall the embarrassment I felt on being told to kiss my mother, or an aunt. Yet throughout my young years I was to feel a deep need, a great longing — but for what? Was it to recapture that intimacy I had with that young girl? Or was it just those sexual hormones kicking in early?

I next wrote about my infant school, the names of the children in my class were written on a big white card, alongside of which stars were stuck, indicating achievement. The stars were in different colours: yellow, red, silver and gold, and I had more than anyone, especially the silver and gold. I must have been rather proud of this, for I can still remember how pleased I felt when, on having been off school for several days — another minor illness — I discovered I still had more stars than any of my fellow pupils.

After a few weeks the creative writing course was cancelled. This occurred shortly after a school inspector had made an assessment — I think it was thought that the tutor should have been teaching us *how* to write, rather than just encouraging us to write. However, it made no difference to me. I was hooked. I was beginning to evaluate my life.

I can't say I've had a bad life. It could have been better, but then, that is true for us all — I am sure, at times, we could all benefit from an analyst, a life-style coach and a personal trainer. But my intention is not to complain of my life, but to examine it with a view to gathering understanding, for, like Horace Walpole, I do not understand anything until I have written it down.

So, what has my life been *about*? What have I *learnt*? What do I think of the ever-changing world I find myself in? We travel to broaden our horizon, but the most interesting and important journey we *all* make, is our journey through *life*. I shall therefore begin at the beginning.

Two

Jack, a young man from a big family, left school at the age of thirteen and then, unable to find work, took up cat-burglary. On arresting him, the police remarked on his daring, one slip would have meant certain death on the railings below. The judge, however, was not so admiring, and for stealing "tomfoolery" Jack spent three Christmases "inside" — sewing mailbags. As this was an occupation, he was not eager to pursue, on his release he took up house painting, and later, decorating.

Bella grew up in Plymouth; left school at fourteen, and at the age of seventeen went to live with an aunt in Shepherd's Bush. She soon found places to work and ended up in a laundry in Acton, where she met Jack's sister, Iris. Before long, Jack and Bella were friends, and on discovering they had "a little bun in the oven" decided to get married. It was not to be a happy union, for my father never allowed my mother to work outside the home ever again, she consequently become friendless and isolated.

"Shepherd's Bush" sounds nice and rural and perhaps once it was, but when I was delivered at Du Cane Road Hospital, there were no longer any shepherds, nor any bushes. Instead, like any metropolitan area, there were only roads and houses. We lived for a short time in two places but then settled into a house in Adelaide Grove, which might suggest trees, but there were none of those either.

When the war started, other people moved out of the house and my parents became sitting tenants. We lived in the basement, which had a bedroom, living room and a small kitchen. The kitchen contained only a sink, a gas cooker and a tiny kitchen cabinet. Much, much later, my father was to install a bath. There was also a little garden.

My father let the first floor to a mother and her young son — he was to share my bedroom, which was also on the first floor. The second floor and attic, was let to a family of four. My parents collected the rent and passed it on to the landlord.

When the war started, I was given a gas mask, shown how to put it on, and then escorted towards a gas-filled truck. Was it the triumphant antics of those that emerged that alarmed me, or was it the usher who urged me to go in alone? Whatever it was, I was having none of it, I didn't know about the gas, but I could sense that there might be some danger and I tore off the mask and screamed — I was not the bravest of children.

During the war, my father kept rabbits and chickens in the back garden; in those times of food rationing they were extra protein. We also had a black dog with a curly tail — my grandfather would threaten to dock its tail with a big knife, and I would protest vigorously.

I loved my dog and would take him on long walks. When I took him to the vet, I was asked how his bowels were, and on my answering, the veterinary surgeon turned to his assistant and expressed surprise that "one so young" should know what "bowels" meant. It broke my heart when the dog had to be "put down" — for some reason that was never explained.

My paternal grandparents lived next door, and it was there, on Bank Holidays, that several members of the family would gather; then drinks would be drunk and cards would be played. I loved these occasions; first I would play my grandfather shove-halfpenny, and then I would be allowed to play pontoon with the rest of the adults until my bedtime. Regrettably, these gatherings did not survive my grandfather's death; he died in 1950.

Air raids were noisy affairs: first the sirens, then the aircraft, then the constant pom-pom-pom of the anti-aircraft "ack-ack" fire. It didn't seem quite real to me. Then one day I saw my teacher comforting a boy whose parents had just been killed; that night, as I lay in bed, I wondered what I would do, if one, or both of my parents, were killed. I tried to imagine the house collapsing on me, would I survive? If not, what would death be like?

Of course, with no first-hand experience of death or injury, such fears did not last long and there was great comfort to be had from friends and family. Even when the bombs were dropping, we were seldom alone, and although, from time to time, I could sense fear in other people, I took comfort from the cosy intimacy that prevailed.

One night, however, I thought a bomb might have landed in our back garden. I was crouched under the kitchen table with my mother — my father had assured us that this, or under the stairs, was the safest place — when suddenly there was an immense boom, the ground shook and the windows shattered. The curtains kept the glass at bay, but where had the bomb landed?

The next morning, I could hardly wait to see the damage, but although I visited all the nearby streets, I could find nothing. The bomb had landed some quarter of a mile away and had removed a whole block from an estate called the Peabody Buildings — I suppose it must have been a V1 Flying Bomb, which was nicknamed a "Doodlebug".

These pilot-less aircrafts were full of high explosives and could be identified by the low-throbbing drone of their engines. On hearing one cut out, we would hold our breath, knowing that somebody was "going to get it". Later in the war, V2s descended. These were rocket-propelled ballistic missiles — there was no air raid warning, no engine was heard, just the explosion.

How I cried on learning I would have to wear glasses. I had recently started primary school, and nothing as traumatic had happened to me since I was circumcised. I clearly remember the circumcision because the end of the bandage stuck to what was left of my little member, and the nurse, no doubt considering this a trifling matter, detached it suddenly — the bandage that is, not my little member. On subsequent visits, my protestations made sure that only I would unwind the bandage. However, circumcision is private; spectacles are public, and my vanity, plus the appellation "four eyes", deterred me from wearing my specs anywhere except in the classroom.

One my favourite activities at primary school was "defending the bench". The bench was attached to a wall in the playground and was defended by boys standing upon it. To attack the bench, you leapt up, threw off one of the defenders and took his place. I now wish I had shown as much enthusiasm for the school lessons as I did for fun and games, but apart from my "minor protest", I did not see the need.

One day my teacher was shocked to learn that I could not spell the name of my own street and she threatened me with the cane should I not be able spell it the following day. On my way home, I stopped at the corner of my street and studied the nameplate, A-D-E-L-A-I-D-E G-R-O-V-E. I was so glad not to be living in the street nearby — Bloemfontein Road. I was caned the following day anyway — for talking during a lesson.

Broad steps led up to the first-floor porch of my house and it was here that me and my mates would often play draughts, or five stones, or perhaps just sit and talk. We were never bored, there were always games to play — marbles, fag-cards, conkers, hop-scotch, tin can alley, football... I never wanted to leave the street either for meals or toilet (the consequential constipation meant having to go to hospital for an enema).

Not even whooping cough could keep me indoors, although I still remember one particularly long, drawn-out *whoop,* when I feared I would *never* get my breath back, but as soon as I did, I was off chasing the ball once again. Incidentally, I seemed to catch most of the germs that were going around then: German measles, ringworm, chicken pox and boils — I had them all, especially the boils.

Coal, milk, fruit and veg' were all delivered by horse and cart. We hardly ever saw a car. Most people could not afford one, and during the war there was petrol rationing, so the streets became children's playgrounds. One of my many pleasures was hurtling up and down the street on my scooter. Homemade scooters were made from planks of wood with ball-bearing races for wheels. In those days, many things were homemade, either by individuals, or by a local community of fathers, brothers and mates.

The only source of entertainment at home was the radio, so from time to time I would try to stay up late, hoping to see my father. He would sometimes arrive home from the pub in an expansive, talkative mood; he was then a good raconteur and would boast of his, and his friends', dodgy dealings.

My parents were not cruel, but at times, a little thoughtless, especially my father. I remember my father crying out in despair that he and my mother could not get out of bed — the door was locked, and I thought they both had polio; it was prevalent at the time. I cried and prayed outside their door until my father indicated it was a joke! On another occasion, I was asked whom I would choose, my mother or my father, if they were to separate!

It is surprising how one can remember even little acts of kindness. I still remember a complete stranger, a Scotsman, who, when he saw me playing in the street, promised me a top — the top was duly given and I had much pleasure with it. Then there were the Yanks. They looked so smart in their uniforms, and my friends would run after them, shouting, "Got any gum, chum?" — but not me, I was too shy. However, on the one occasion when my parents sought shelter down the Underground, a Yank gave me a bar of chocolate, which he got from a vending machine.

In today's affluent society, such little acts of kindness would go unnoticed, but I still remember the Scotsman and the Yank. I do so hope the Yank survived the war; giving me a bar of chocolate was a tiny gesture, but risking life and limb in a war so far from home: that seems an immense act of generosity.

Incidentally, the experience of sheltering down the Underground was not to be repeated. We found people spread all over the platforms like sardines, and when my mother woke up with somebody's feet in her face, she decided that in future she would rather risk Hitler's bombs than a pair of sweaty feet.

Three

Sometimes, when "flush" with money, my father would give my mother a few extra quid so she could treat herself — she never did. Instead, she salted it away for clothes or emergencies. Later, when my father was broke, he would discover my mother's cache, and a row would erupt. On at least one occasion he even stole my meagre savings, not that he would have regarded any of this as stealing, for as the sole breadwinner, all money came from him, so any surplus should surely be his when he needed it.

Although my father wasted much of his money in the pub and betting shop, he could, when circumstances pressed, be thrifty. When my mother complained that she had no sunglasses, my father had a solution — he varnished an old pair of my mother's reading glasses. My mother happily spent all day in the sun, but overdid it. Her face became lobster red, and when she took off her glasses, her albino eyes looked so comical that she refused to leave the house for days. On another occasion, my father knocked a square hole in a plaster wall that divided the bedroom from the dining room; this enabled him to hear the relay radio in both rooms!

Such poverty made me parsimonious. When a friend's mother took her son Harry and me to Ramsgate, my reluctance to gamble my money on the "roll a penny" at the funfair gave rise to some humorous comments about my penny pinching. But then I was a sensitive kid and perhaps took my self-denial too far. When my mates decided we should all wear distinctive string-vests to denote that we all belonged to the same gang, I could not bring myself to ask my parents to buy one for me, not out of fear, but out of consideration — I was constantly aware that money was scarce. Eventually, my mates asked my father, and I got the string vest.

My mother loved the cinema and she took me with her at least once a week. I also loved the cinema, especially the gangster movies. George Raft, Edward G. Robinson, James Cagney — I loved them all. The characters James Cagney portrayed visibly influenced one of the boys in my class and I wondered whether it was this influence that brought him to the attention of the police.

Do films influence the way people choose to live? One would not expect children brought up in a discerning, academic environment to be adversely affected — such children have no need to break the law to achieve *their* goals, they know *their* future will be bright and secure.

Four

I suppose being a member of a street gang toughened me up somewhat, for I was not naturally brave. In fact, I always felt a little different from my mates, not quite so rough or so crude. I did not usually swear, and when I did, it would shock everybody, and I was reluctant to get into mischief. When my friend, Charlie, shoplifted in Woolworth's, I would look the other way, and it was only peer pressure that forced me to sneak into a cinema without paying (after a mate, who had paid, opened the back door).

Again, peer pressure demanded that a disagreement with David, another gang member, had to be settled by the "noble art" and as we had no boxing gloves, our hands were wrapped with bandages — which were a poor substitute! However, without my mates, life would have been dull, they made things happen. Left alone, I was a docile child. My parents had no problems with me, and I did as I was told.

I was told to be polite and considerate; to give up my seat to women and not to swear in front of them; adults had to be respected and deferred to. I never warranted any punishment apart from the occasional clip round the ear. My friend Charlie, on the other hand, was rather mischievous and rebellious, and his father would take a strap to him. Dr Spock's advice was not current at the time. The prevailing aphorisms were "spare the rod and spoil the child" or "keep their bowels open and their mouths shut".

Charlie was almost two years older than I, and when he got a paper round I would keep him company and would make up stories to tell him. I was a good story teller; one of my characters was a granite statue that "came to life" whenever it spotted a crime; and there were other stories involving a gang of kids — I suspected that Charlie identified with one called Nobby, so I made this character the most colourful.

Had it not been for Charlie I would never have owned three guns — two revolvers and an automatic. He had stolen them from an armoury on Wormwood Scrubs. All the guns were minus their firing pins, so they were quite harmless, although nowadays one realises that this isn't necessarily so. Incidentally, I have no idea what happened to the guns or to the many other things that passed through my hands — I suppose all kids are the same, with all manner of things being bought and bartered.

Gang members came and went over the years; the older members found jobs and some others moved away. There were never more than about eight of us and then not for very long. A boy called Harry White was one of my closest friends because we had spent many evenings together waiting for our parents to come home from the pub. There were never any girls around.

Five

Neither myself, nor any of my friends, were evacuated, nor did any of us pass the 11-plus. My cousin John, who lived next door, was evacuated, and he was looked after by two retired schoolteachers who wanted to adopt him. My grandparents resisted the adoption, but on his return, he was never allowed to play with us street urchins; we thought such boys were sissies — but it was John that passed his 11-plus.

Hammersmith Secondary School was within sight of Wormwood Scrubs Prison. One might have thought this would have acted as a deterrent to bad behaviour, but apparently, it made no difference, for during morning assembly the headmaster would often complain that too many of us were becoming known to the police.

Fights were commonplace, sometimes for the most trivial reasons. One day, on walking with two younger friends in East Acton, I was surrounded by a dozen or more boys. "That's him," someone shouted. Suddenly I was hit in the face and my lip was busted. Apparently, I had hit some kid in the playground with a snowball, and his gang were taking revenge! We escaped by running for a bus. Sometimes, after a fight or an angry incident, I was afraid of going to school the next day for fear of being beaten up. But I always did go, and I never did get beaten up — hostilities were soon forgotten.

If you wanted to survive with some respect, however, it was important to assess your position in the pecking order and to maintain that position. I remember feeling obliged to defend a young boy named George. He was a small lad with fair hair and although too young to be a friend, he was a neighbour. I tried to remonstrate with his attacker, a boy from my own class, but he was not prepared to back down in front of his mates, so we both had to fight or lose face.

All boys love to watch a good fight, and almost immediately, a circle of boys were cheering us on. A prefect broke up the fight and he took us to see the headmaster. The headmaster was not in his room, so we were told to wait for him. Of course, we didn't. Instead we returned to our class where we enjoyed telling our friends what had happened. My opponent and I had a mutual respect for each other after that.

However, I was not brave. I tried to keep a low profile. There were forty-four boys in my class, and we all knew our place in the pecking order, so when I fell foul of Baker, one of the toughest boys in the school, it felt so unreal. It started during a woodwork class; strips of veneer were stored on the floor between two cupboards, and I was crouching down, trying to decide which would best complement my lamp standard. Suddenly, I was sent sprawling. "Out of my way, Dorrell," Baker had kneed me and I felt a surge of anger.

Although docile, I seem to have been born with a strong sense of justice and injustice. At infants' school, I always made sure of getting my free milk, and at primary school, I was outraged at being wrongly accused of sending a note to one of the girls in my class — and being caned for it!

Another injustice occurred in the art class at my secondary school. I was very good at art, but then, so was Peter, a big boy who lived in the top flat of my house. A painting competition had taken place, and the class decided I was the winner. I was given a second-hand book as a prize. Peter was incensed, for he thought he should have won and he persuaded the "judges" to change their minds. I didn't argue, I just flew out of the classroom with my prize, and Peter chased me all the way home.

However, I am digressing. My sense of outrage at being wantonly kneed out of way by Baker had evoked anger. Beside me was a tool rack, and from it I removed a big screwdriver; holding it by its tip, I made as if to throw it as a knife. Suddenly, Baker turned around — someone had shouted a warning. He stared at me in disbelief. He then slowly walked towards me, took the screwdriver from my hand and said, "I'll see you outside, Dorrell."

That seemed like a death sentence. I was terrified, but "face" was everything, and I tried to appear unconcerned. My friends were solicitous; others less so.

"Baker's going to kill you, Dorrell," one boy whispered.

"Piss off," I retorted, but I was feeling far from brave. This was such a bizarre situation, I was not a big boy, and I was not tough, my reaction had been no more than a melodramatic gesture. I was even relieved that Baker had turned around when he did, I would have felt rather foolish replacing the screwdriver myself. But now I was in serious trouble: my heart was pounding and my guts were knotted in fear.

Could I run away? I knew I couldn't. I had fallen foul of Baker once before. On that occasion I had tried to outrun him

— I was fast, but I lacked stamina — I just managed to make it around a corner, and then, like an animal at bay, I hid. Baker soon found me, and then he and his friends carried me off like some trophy of war. They then discussed whether or not to throw me in the canal. I tried to appeal to their better natures, their sense of fair play, their friendship; I remonstrated with torrents of words — and they let me go!

Could I, again, talk myself out of it? What could I say? What were the alternatives: perhaps if I struck first and kicked him in the balls? No, I knew I could never do that. Suddenly the bell rang — it was time to leave. I moved like a zombie towards the exit. The stairs were full of departing boys — there was no escape. Then I felt a hand on my shoulder, it was Baker's, "I'm letting you off this time, Dorrell, but don't ever cross me again." I never found out why he let me off.

I shudder to think what happens in a rough school nowadays; I never saw a knife used, and if we were ever cruel or mean, it was seldom excessive. In many ways, I suppose I was fortunate. We all spoke the same language, had the same working class culture and there were no drugs and no muggings. We might have challenged authority, but we also respected it — and the cane was used liberally.

But of course, back then, the moral climate was different; I suppose it was the war. The war had produced a nation that was used to self-sacrifice, discipline and responsibility. Moreover, there was a morality based on strong Christian ethics; in those days, religion may have been ignored, questioned or criticised, but it was always there, a *spectre*, forming judgements.

Six

Rows between my mother and father were frequent before, during and after the war, either over money, or because my mother was lonely and never taken anywhere. My father's idea of giving my mother a good time was to take her to the pub, sit her down with a drink, and then return to his cronies at the bar. Bank Holidays and Christmases were the worst; plans would be made to "go somewhere", and then Dad would get drunk and spoil it all. I hated the scenes that followed and would go for long walks. Sometimes my mother's temper got the better of her, and on one occasion she removed my father's front teeth with a well-aimed plate. "The doctor said I was a hero for not retaliating," my father boasted. I don't remember this incident, so it must have happened when I was very young.

My father had no social aspirations and was critical of all those that had — his aspiring brothers were "tight-fisted", or "under the thumbs of their wives" — consequently, although my father had lots of brothers and sisters, he was close to none. Within the family he was considered a bit of a black sheep, but with a poor education and a prison record, wasn't he hobbled for life? I imagine the only way he felt he could live with any shred of dignity was to embrace the macho working class way of life — to drink, gamble, and take no shit from anyone — in such an environment his prison record would have given him prestige.

However, I believe away from his work mates and pub cronies, my father was socially inadequate, especially when dealing with his middle class clients, and this impression was given greater clarity later in my life, when, on a visit to the seaside, he refused to enter a café with me, my girlfriend, and my mother. Why? Because it was waitress service, and no amount of persuasion would change his mind. I sometimes wondered if it was his social inadequacy that caused him to drink so much.

My parents never mentioned religion, but at times, one couldn't escape the feeling that one was being judged from on high. When Frankie Laine sang, "*I Believe*", it was not too difficult for me to believe as well. But then my critical faculty would take over: how could God expect everybody to worship Him when most of the world's population had never even heard of Him? What about other religions? Their adherents were equally convinced that *their* God was the only *true* God. And what about all those prayers and hymns: wouldn't any intelligent God be sick to his back teeth with all that praise and adulation?

Seven

I wish I could look back on my school days with some sense of achievement, but for me, and I suspect for many of my mates, education did not lead to enlightenment, but to indifference — school was something to get through until we could leave and start work. Even so, I was top of my class in art and arithmetic, and pretty good at woodwork, but an inability to spell, and an inadequate vocabulary, made English difficult.

When the English teacher asked us to write an account of our journey to school, my essay included the words "worse luck" — it was my response to having been asked by a friend "Where are you going?" "To school", I replied, "worse luck" — the teacher put his pen across it and wrote, "Terrible English." Of course it was — that was how I spoke. I was very resentful. I thought he was unjust to criticise my "reported speech", as I felt I was being authentic. Back then, of course, I was too inarticulate to have expressed such a view.

Hammersmith Secondary School had some good and bad teachers. One of the good ones read us *Wind in the Willows* and *Macbeth*; we listened dutifully — anything better than class "work" — and when he read us stories from Damon Runyon, we listened attentively. This teacher even put on a classical play in which a man escaped from prison by dressing up as a woman. Our enthusiasm for this production may have arisen from the belief that such knowledge might one day come in useful.

Another teacher took the class to Wormwood Scrubs Common. We were told to sit down and draw the nearby trees. I was rather proud of my artistic ability, and I produced a very delicate drawing showing a fine tracery of branches and individual leaves, rather like a Constable. This young teacher, who usually taught PT, was no art teacher. He peered at my work and said I should be bold; he then drew thick lines all over it.

On another occasion, this same teacher had seen me fashioning a boat out of wood. He then took both the wood and penknife from me and proceeded to gouge out the upper deck. "What sort of boat is it?" he asked.

"A galleon," I replied. He laughed.

"I thought it was a rowing boat," said he, thrusting the wood and penknife back into my hands. He then looked to the other boys for approval. None of them laughed — it had been a mean joke, and I felt quite touched by their tacit support.

In retrospect, I can understand why this teacher was so mean; he was very young and no doubt thought it necessary to create a tough image, for maintaining discipline was far from easy. One teacher, on struggling to maintain control over his class, broke a wooden ruler over a boy's head. I think it shook the teacher as much as the rest of us, but he carried on as though nothing untoward had occurred. Any sign of weakness would have given us licence for more disruptive behaviour.

Our English teacher was a big balding man with a ruddy complexion. I remember him striding between rows of desks reciting:

There's a breathless hush in the close tonight,
Ten to make and the match to win.

He was a good teacher, but even he was driven to violence. On receiving insolence from the biggest boy in the class, he told the boy to stand up. The boy was over six foot tall, broad-shouldered, and tough, we were all scared of him. I did not hear what the boy said, but the teacher punched him in the stomach and he collapsed into his seat in pain.

I was astonished, and the class was stunned into silence; but the teacher had maintained his authority, and our respect. Some teachers could do neither. One broke down in tears on failing to control an unruly class, and I viewed the spectacle with a mixture of pity and contempt. That teacher lacked authority. He had tried various ways to maintain discipline, including entreaty and the cane, but he was weak and therefore vulnerable.

On another occasion, this same teacher became involved in a violent struggle with a small boy he was trying to eject from the school. The teacher was quite small himself and was having considerable difficulty, but he eventually managed to drag the boy down the steps and into the playground by his legs. The boy had a hot temper and a bad reputation, he immediately sprang to his feet, ran up to the retreating teacher and delivered a two-fisted blow to the back of the teacher's neck. The boy was expelled — I don't know what happened to the teacher. Incidentally, the English teacher, soon after the punching incident, went on to teach at a public school, so his career did not suffer.

I am aware that these incidents seem very dramatic, and I suppose that is why they have stuck in my memory, but overall, school was not such a bad place. In fact, I feel nothing but gratitude towards those teachers that did manage to teach me something. Throughout my life I have recalled *some* of the knowledge they were trying to impart — the magnets and ferrous filings, the arithmetic and poetry — I regret not having been more attentive at the time.

Eight

I didn't know anyone who took religious education seriously, but some of it stuck, and the questions about good and evil, and life after death, are never entirely forgotten. I enjoyed singing the hymns, especially *Jerusalem* and *I Vow to Thee My Country* and the Bible contained some jolly good verses:

Whither thou goest, I will go; and where thou lodgest, I will lodge: thy people shall be my people, and thy God my God: where thou diest, I will die, and there will I be buried.

Or,

When I was a child, I spoke as a child, I understood as a child, I thought as a child: but when I became a man, I put away childish things. For now we see as through a glass, darkly; but then face to face.

This enlivens the brain and touches the spirit — I think the Bible should be taught as literature. My quotations are from the King James Version. I doubt whether the New English Bible would inspire quite the same passion.

My friends and I never gave much thought about what we would do on leaving school — we were just eager to leave, earn some money, and "be grown up". I had assumed I would follow in my father's footsteps — painting and decorating. However, when the time drew near, my father said, "You don't want to get into my game, son — it's too hard." Therefore, with less than a month to go before leaving school, I had no idea of what work to seek, but the state had plans for pupils like me:

We were all squatting in the assembly hall and were being addressed by a careers advisor, "I am not going to give you a load of bullshit." he said, "You're not going to be architects or accountants, but the country needs good labourers — people not afraid of getting their hands dirty." This was my epiphany — we had all been consigned to the scrap heap! I don't know why this came as a revelation — after all, what more could I have reasonably expected?

Soon after this we were then taken on an industrial visit to an engineering factory in Willesden, where we were shown the lathes and other machines before being interviewed in the office. A motherly, caring woman looked at me closely, "Are you *sure* this is the kind of work you want?" I nodded my head. When I was offered the job my father said, "You don't want that, it's too far away."

I then attended the Youth Careers Office. "Have you any idea what sort of work you would like, young man?" the woman asked.

"I have always wanted to be a printer," I said. It was a sudden impulse, I had heard somewhere, that printers earn lots of money.

She looked a little surprised. "You're a very lucky young man, a job as an apprentice in the printing trade has just come in."

Nine

My employment was with a small firm in Holland Park: there was a manager, an auxiliary worker, a part-time book-binder, a linotype operator, a compositor, an apprentice compositor, a machine minder, an apprentice machine minder (who was soon to do his National Service) and me, I was to be another apprentice machine minder.

My working day was 8 a.m. to 5.30 p.m. I would start by making a list of what the other workers wanted for their mid-morning tea break and would then take the order to the local café. The café was run by an old man and his wife, and on sipping my tea, I would observe the daily routine of a husband struggling vainly to keep up with the demands of a wife who was never satisfied. He cowered over his duties as his wife constantly berated him, and apart from the odd bleat, was fearful of answering back. I realised I was watching a man who had been broken by years of hen-pecking.

At lunchtime, I was sent to buy fish and chips, and standing in the queue, and there always was a queue, I would be puzzled by the notice, "Please do not ask for credit as denial often offends." I was puzzled, as I could only think of "credit as meaning "praise"! Every day the same old faces would appear: smoking, roller-haired women, dressed in slippers and dressing-gowns. I would wonder about their husbands: were they indifferent to their wives' appearance, or did they leave their wives in bed each morning and return in the evening to find these women had miraculously managed to transform themselves?

The "chippy" was just around the corner from 10 Rillington Place. This was where John Reginald Halliday Christie had lived; Christie would pick up women in a local pub and then lure them back to his house on the pretext that he had a remedy for any breathing problems they might have. His "cure," was an inhaler. It always worked, they never had breathing problems afterwards — his inhaler was connected to the gas main! I cannot remember how many cures he accomplished, but the bodies were concealed all over the house and garden. After the trial, the house was demolished.

Incidentally, many of us had breathing difficulties in those days. *A foggy day in London Town* might be a romantic song, but a winter fog often became a smog (which was fog polluted by the smoke and sulphur of domestic coal fires), and "a smoggy day in London Town" was far from romantic — in December 1952, London smog killed four thousand people.

I sometimes wonder how many people died on the top deck of a London trolley bus — for the pollution there must have been just as lethal as London smog — for it was the smoker's deck. When the lower deck was full, I would have no alternative but to go "on top where a thick pall of blue smoke would sting my eyes as I groped to find a seat. Sitting in the toxic fug I would hear the sounds of lungs struggling to clear phlegm. The trolley bus clippie must have hated it.

My working environment was dingy, dirty and noisy. I seldom saw the light of day because the machine shop was in a basement. By comparison, the composing department was a refuge of tranquillity, it was quieter and overlooked a beautiful garden. Had I the choice I would have preferred working as an apprentice compositor, but Fred, a man who had just returned from National Service, had that job.

I found the work soulless and monotonous; one day frantically stapling the weekly magazine — there was always a sense of urgency — and most other days feeding the printing press. This greedy giant was hand fed, one sheet at a time, and would gobble up ream after ream of paper. Feeding that machine hour after hour was hell. I used to think, should this ever become a penal punishment, prisons would soon be empty, for no one would want to return.

From time to time the press would need a change of ink and I would wash the rollers with paraffin. Afterwards, I would scrub my hands raw to get the ink off them. Another of my jobs was to melt down the slugs that had been produced by the linotype machines. I would carry the slugs to the garden shed, where there was a crucible, and on melting them down would ladle the molten metal into iron moulds.

On even the warmest of days the moulds must have been damp, for the hot lead would fly up and attack my arms and face — it was the only time I was glad to be wearing glasses. I would then carry the ingots back to the linotype room, where they could be used once again to produce lines of type.

I enjoyed the hard, physical work, but found the fumes unpleasant and would cover my face with a handkerchief. Of course, gloves and a mask would have made it more acceptable, but back then such things were not given any consideration. At the end of each day I would sweep the floors and gather up all the waste paper. There were three types of waste paper: white, coloured, and waste, and each had to be put in separate sacks and stored in the crucible shed in the garden.

I was supposed to learn my trade from the machine minder: he was an old boy in his seventies, cantankerous and short on temper. He explained nothing, I could only watch. I think he saw me as a threat, and that by teaching me he might put himself out of a job. The one thing I did learn was chess. The linotype operator taught me, and within a few weeks I was beating him.

I thought I must be quite good. "I hear you play chess. Would you give me a game?" The request came from the young boy I was baby-sitting. I felt rather superior. Did this little boy really want to play *me*? He seemed so keen I felt it would be cruel to disappoint him. He thrashed me repeatedly. He was well versed in all tactics and strategy, while I had never even heard of fool's mate! It was a bitter lesson; natural talent was no substitute for thorough teaching — the boy's father was a chess enthusiast.

Ten

Perhaps I made my apprenticeship sound a little too grim. I can't say it was a pleasure, but there were agreeable moments, and although my fellow workers were not strong on conversation, most were pleasant enough. Moreover, printing was rather an interesting trade: the different papers and inks, the various typefaces, and a whole new language to learn: points, en's, picas; galleys, chaises and quoins; folios, quartos, octavos, and many, many more.

Most of our printing was for a spiritualist society, the headquarters of which was upstairs. None of my fellow workers believed in spiritualism, and most of the spiritualists were very old, but when I heard them singing their hymns in the chapel above and contrasted it with the profanity at my level, I could scarcely rid myself of the notion that upstairs was the holier place.

Before long, I discovered dozens of copper half-tone plates which showed pictures of women with babies. The babies were not in their mothers' arms, but could be seen emerging from a little cloud above the mother's head — sometimes it wasn't a baby, but a child, or even an adult. I was intrigued and sufficiently curious to learn a little more about spiritualism.

In the early twentieth century, its advocates included: Lord Dowding, William Crooks, a scientist, and Sir Arthur Conan Doyle an author. Had these eminent people been bamboozled? Later in my life, I was to realise that even a specialist outside his or her field of expertise is just as likely to believe in nonsense as the rest of us. On reading of the paraphernalia of dark rooms, floating lights and ectoplasm, I realised the conditions were perfect for fraudulent behaviour.

I had a lot of respect for my friend Bill. He had attended a grammar school and his parents owned the local sweet shop, so if Bill was entirely convinced, could there be something in it? Bill had had a weird experience with an Ouija board. He had sat at a table with his sister and two other people, and each had placed their little finger on top of a glass.

A spiritual presence was then summoned and questioned, whereupon the glass moved to letters and numbers that had been arranged around the table. Bill was to learn that he would not die before the age of eighty-five. He was convinced that nobody had pushed the glass, for their fingers had barely touched it. The glass just glided over the table "mysteriously". I was suspicious, but silent. Had Bill's sister arranged the Ouija experience in order to reassure Bill that he would not meet an early death like his father?

I was to read, some years later, that the trick was to heat the glass beforehand, and then, once the glass was placed on a polished surface, the heated air trapped inside would practically hover the glass and require only the gentlest of nudges to steer it.

One of my favourite jobs was folding the printed sheets of paper by hand. Usually the printed sheets were folded by machine, but for small quantities, hand folding was more convenient as the folding machine did not have to be reset.

This job gave me opportunity to sit alone in the backroom; there I could enjoy the daylight, the peace and the quiet.

One day, on folding a spiritualist periodical, I noticed some poetry. Most poetry passed over my head, but on this occasion, there were two stanzas that caught my eye. Only they belonged to two different poems, written by two different authors. I decided they should be put together, to form a single poem.

They think I am always happy, because I wear a smile
But all is on the surface; my heart aches all the while
But still I must laugh and chatter and with the world move on
Whilst hugging close my secret of happiness that's gone

There! Were not those two stanzas made for each other? I thought they were.

During this first year of my apprenticeship, I had a regular girlfriend, Betty Brooks. I had met Betty at a night school dance. We did a lot of snogging and no doubt would have gone further had the opportunity arose, but Betty's porch hardly seemed the appropriate place. Perhaps this was fortuitous, for in those days snogging invariably led to sex, sex led to babies, babies led to marriage, and marriage led to poverty. The whole idea of being pressured into marriage must nowadays sound awfully quaint, but in those days, birth control was not easy, and abortion was a crime. We talked about living together in a nice little house, but I was aware we were only fantasising. I had a seven-year apprenticeship to complete and I was earning a pittance, most of which I was giving to my mother. I soon realised that Betty and I had very little in common.

Eleven

On my way to and from work I would pass a second-hand book shop. I can still remember the thrill of reading *Life of a Super Tramp* by W. H. Davies and I was to discover later that Davies wrote one of my favourite poems, *Leisure.* My choices of reading were very hit and miss, but when I discovered something of interest, I found it so very worthwhile.

On a Saturday morning I would sometimes visit my local library, but I was not very clever at making the most of it — so many books: which to choose? I had no idea. I would always look at those on the display table, but they were invariably romantic novels, but I eventually discovered a section that contained plays, and the plays of Bernard Shaw and Oscar Wilde became my favourites.

Nowadays, one is spoilt for choice, there is so much to amuse and inspire: CDs, videos, television. On first hearing about television, I was incredulous; how could it possibly work? How could a moving picture travel though space? At the time, of course, landing on the moon and a computer in every home would have been the stuff of science fiction.

Sometimes, I went swimming, there were good pools at Bloemfontein Road and Lime Grove, but on one occasion I went to Porchester Hall, where I saw very young boys jumping off the high diving board. Well, if they could do it, it must be easy. I climbed up the metal ladder and inched my way to the end of the board. My God, I wasn't aware of how flexible it would be! I looked down. My God! The pool seemed so far down, I felt giddy. I would have to go back. I turned around, there was a young boy at the other end of the board and several more were clinging to the ladder — they were all staring at me, impatiently awaiting their turn. I was trapped! I made a painful belly flop.

It has occurred to me that up until now, I have never mentioned food; all I can say is: thank God for school dinners. School dinners may not have been especially appetising, but they provided a balanced diet, and some of the puddings were delicious. On leaving school my diet was rubbish — "five helpings of fruit and veg every day? I never had that much in a week. I suppose that's why I frequently suffered from colds and boils. Except for the Sunday roast, which my father would cook, I can scarcely remember looking forward to any meals at home, but my mother was good at baking cakes and the occasional rice pudding.

At work I would buy three crusty rolls, some processed cheese triangles and some chips. On scooping out the insides of the rolls I would stuff them with the cheese and chips and then put them on one of the coke fires that provided the central heating. After half an hour, the rolls would be hot, crispy and delicious.

One day my employer sent me to the London School of Printing. On arrival, we were taken around the school, shown the classrooms and told what would be expected of us during the following year. I was over the moon, at last I would have the opportunity to learn. I looked forward to it eagerly. The next day I told my manager how much I appreciated being sent to the school. "Oh, you are not going. They have increased the attendance from half-a-day to one full day a week. We cannot spare you for a whole day." I was devastated.

Twelve

Burglary is not something one should undertake lightly, so why did I decide on such an extreme measure? At the time I had been reading a book about Raffles, but this hardly seems an adequate explanation. Money? I certainly had very little; on the other hand, I was not materialistic and had learned to live frugally. No, in the last analysis, it was frustration and anger; I had wanted an opportunity to prove and improve myself, but was getting nowhere fast. When I shared my intention with a friend, he liked the idea and even suggested a place we might break into — a private dance hall.

We were to climb over a back wall and into the garden. From there we would gain a quiet entry into the building by spreading treacle and brown paper over a windowpane before breaking it — was this a Raffles idea? However, when we arrived at the chosen place, we found children were playing football in front of the very garden wall we were planning to climb over. We walked around the block a few times, but the children were still there, even up to midnight. We took this as a bad omen and thought that anyway, we had made ourselves too conspicuous.

We never did try again. How many doors might have closed had we done so — and got caught! At the time the prospect of getting caught did not frighten me, as I thought I could work the system; it would have been my first offence, I would be all contrite and full of excuses and would no doubt escape with a warning, or perhaps, probation. How naïve! I never gave a thought as to how a criminal record might have fucked up the rest of my life.

After that, I tried to improve my printing knowledge by attending evening classes at the London School of Printing. Who was it that said, "Night school is a place where tired teachers teach tired students"? Our tutor was an old man, he would reminisce about his previous experience and then convey to us his antiquated advice — all of which I dutifully noted down. Whenever he tested our knowledge, I shone. On sitting the City and Guilds, however, I was in shock; I could scarcely answer any of the questions.

I was by then so utterly disillusioned and frustrated that I told my manager that I was tired of being treated like a skivvy and that I wanted to break my apprenticeship.

"You can't," he said, "you are bound by the terms and conditions of your indentures"

I was defiant. "What if I leave a spanner in the works?"

He was shocked and then conciliatory. He told me I would soon be called up for National Service and that this would count towards the completion of my apprenticeship, effectively reducing it from seven years to five. "You will then," he said, "be able to earn a decent wage."

During this period, I belonged to a boys' club where I played snooker and table tennis — do they still have boys' clubs, I wonder? I was segregated from girls at school and seemed segregated again at play. Was this a deliberate policy or was I just unlucky? In order to cope with my increasing frustrations, I took up weightlifting and boxing. — I had wanted to box during my last months at school, but the facilities were withdrawn.

Until recently, I was convinced that Kirk Douglas inspired me to take up boxing after seeing the film *The Champion.* But having recently seen the film again, this hardly seems plausible, for at the end of the film Kirk dies of a brain haemorrhage after having taken a terrific beating in the ring. Had I wanted to impress my father? I did sometimes feel I might have been a disappointment to him — not on his wavelength — perhaps not tough enough. Or was I trying to prove something to myself?

My first fight was at a working men's club in East Acton — the local newspaper reported it in glowing terms, "this boy has a promising future," but then my opponent, like myself, was a complete novice. When I fought at Lime Grove, I met a more seasoned boxer; he hit me in the solar plexus and badly winded me. I fought on, but he had me down repeatedly, and the fight was stopped before I wore out the canvas. At my third venue, my opponent did not show up, and I had to go into the ring against a substitute. He had had over a hundred fights, and I could not land a glove on him, but he had no such difficulty in hitting me.

After that I concentrated on weightlifting. I went three times a week after work. The only food I had beforehand was a pint of gold-topped milk with a raw egg or two. Probably not the best of diets, but I did eventually obtain a first-class Certificate of Merit (for the press and the curl).

Thirteen

Youth culture, when I was young, existed, if at all, only in the shadow of adults — we did what older people did; we dressed much the same, listened to the same music — and ignorance and superstition were handed down from father to son. My only attempt at individuality was to wear bright socks and loud ties.

Authority, whether it took the form of a policeman, schoolteacher or adult, was respected, or at least feared, and one could not escape the feeling that someone was in charge and that justice would be done. There were very few let-out clauses — responsibility stopped at the door of the perpetrator.

Nowadays, it seems a thousand and one excuses can be found for the thief and the brute, but during my teenage years, penalties were severe. We knew Approved Schools and Borstals were tough places, and everyone was aware of the ultimate punishment — the death penalty. The date of an execution would be reported in the press and on the radio, and to most people hanging was seen as justice — a life for a life. But of course, nothing is black and white, and there were some notorious misjudgements.

I well remember the Craig/Bentley case. Christopher Craig shot dead a policeman, but because he was only 16 and too young to hang, his accomplice, Derek Bentley, was hanged instead. Rough justice indeed, especially as the accomplice, aged nineteen, was alleged to have a mental age of only eleven. I was seventeen at the time and I thought the outcome was wrong and scary (on 30th July 1998 an Appeal Court ruled that this conviction had been unsafe).

The last woman to be hanged in England was Ruth Ellis. She shot and killed her lover after losing her baby — her miscarriage had occurred ten days after Blakely, her lover, had beaten her up. She was executed on 13th July 1955.

I sometimes played darts in a pub. There were four of them and only two of us. A tall youth snatched the darts from my hands, threw them, plucked them from the board and then thrust them back towards me. "Throw," it was not so much a request as an order. I threw. Before long, to win, a double was required. I threw and missed. Then a lad from the other team threw, but no sooner had his first dart hit the board than his lanky partner withdrew it. They then demanded a round of drinks. I had seen clearly that no double had been scored — so no drinks would be bought.

The guy who had supposedly thrown the winning dart then challenged me to a fight. He would fight me in the toilet downstairs. I looked him over; he was a short, burly guy, heavier than me, and in a confined space I felt his weight and strength would put me at a distinct disadvantage. I told him there was no way I would fight him in the toilet, but I would be happy to do so outside, in the street. But my alternative venue did not meet with his approval, and as neither of us was prepared to meet the other's terms, we reached deadlock. It soon became clear that my challenger was, in fact, relieved to find a way out — I suspect his friends had pressured him into challenging me.

Another recreation was "going to the dogs". That is, I went to see greyhound racing at the White City Stadium. Once there, my friend and I would pore over the race card and select three cross-win doubles for each race. We bet on the Tote and more times than not we won enough to cover our expenses.

Fourteen

Everybody in the RAF seemed to have "O" levels except me; I can only suppose it was the boxing and weightlifting that got my application past the recruitment panel. It was June 1954 and National Service came as a revelation for I saw a complete cross-section of the British class system: the poor and the posh, the state and public school. Unfortunately, we never had the time or the energy to socialise; after the "square-bashing" and a "passing out parade" we were re-located to positions more in keeping with our abilities and status.

I was to be trained as a radar operator and was sent to Warrington to learn the basics. In order to celebrate our more relaxed regime, Brummie, a little lad from Birmingham, suggested we should go to Manchester. Now everything about Brummie was slow and relaxed. He could take five minutes to cross a road, so I was a little surprised to find he had a very powerful motorbike, a BSA 500.

"Take it easy," I said, "I have never been on the back of one of these things before."

"Oh, you'll be all right," he said. "Just hold on to me and lean over when we take a corner."

No time for second thoughts, we were off like a bat out of hell. At the first corner the bike lurched over sideways and sparks flew from the footrest as it scraped the ground. I looked over Brummie's shoulder, the speedometer reached and surpassed 70 mph and the wind-pressure on my eyelids was such that I could barely keep my eyes open. I was aware Brummie had no goggles. Supposing he gets a fly or something in his eye! I just prayed. I don't remember the return journey at all; alcohol can be such a blessing.

After completing the basic training, I was posted to St. Margaret's Bay, near Dover. In addition to our radar duties we were still undergoing training. One seldom hears the word "awe" nowadays. Perhaps it's the religious connotations, or perhaps it seems somewhat inappropriate in our modern, secular society, or perhaps we have become blasé through living in a constantly innovative, technological world.

Perhaps awe is the wrong word; perhaps it was just amazement born of my lack of education and sophistication, but to this very day I still think the sub-atomic world is amazing. To learn that the universe is held together by eddies of energy in a galaxy of space, really blew my mind. There appears to be a parallel universe beneath the reality of shoes, ships and sealing wax, one so bizarre, that scientists are still trying to figure it out.

Then there is the Periodic Table, less awesome, but still astonishing. I was to learn that everything in the world was made up of ninety-two elements, and one could learn all their names and characteristics — I have since learnt that there are now more than one hundred, but the extra ones are man-made and radioactive. I was even more enthralled, years later, to learn that most of the elements that made life possible have been created in a supernova explosion — one of the most dramatic events in the universe. Knowing this, how can we look at the stars and not feel a sense of awe?

My duties as a radar operator were to keep track of aircraft flying in and out of south-east England. An image of this area was projected from a radar screen onto a large, round, horizontal sheet of glass, and upon this, blips would appear, and then fade, only to reappear a little further away. These blips had to be plotted with a marker pencil after which the information was passed by way of a telephone headset to another person in a control room, where I imagine it was displayed on a large map.

One could see blips (aircraft) making their way across the continent and over the channel and it was up to us radar operators — for there were about five of us — to provide the direction, geographical reference, height and identity. "South-West, Kilo Lima, One Three, Five Six. Kilo Lima, One Three, Five Six. One at Two Three — Allied 249." Fortunately, we never had a "Hostile," but sometimes we had an "Unidentified", and then there was a minor flap if it remained unidentified for too long.

Sometimes these blips would move very slowly, if at all, and then we would discount them as balloons, or they might move at impossible speeds or change direction at impossible vectors, before stopping or disappearing — we called these blips, "Angels". Perhaps today we would have called them UFOs.

The discipline at St. Margaret's during the first few weeks was quite strict. We were virtually confined to camp on the whim of the military police, and I felt it would have been easier to get out of Colditz. When Roger, a friend, suggested we break out through a hole in the fence, I was appalled — but tempted. Why not? Sometimes breaking the rules is a way of expressing one's individuality and freedom.

We got through the barbed wire fence without difficulty and then made our way to the beach where there was a pub called the "The Green Man". The beer was good, but any exhilaration I felt at having exercised a little free will was tempered by the anxiety that an officer might walk in at any moment.

Incidentally, I had a great respect for Roger; he had six "O" levels and an insouciant attitude towards authority that bordered on insolence. An example of this became apparent on the parade ground. A very young pilot officer had been summoned to drill us — a substitute for our formidable sergeant major — and each time he gave an order, Roger would raise his leg and produce a very audible raspberry.

Sex was scarcely discussed, but I dare say we were all sexually frustrated. I know I was. Initially, however, the demands of the training and the films we all had to watch on venereal diseases dampened any sexual urges. Nature, however, will not be denied for long.

We were being shown an old movie in which a beautiful girl kept throwing herself at an emotionally constipated, upper class twit. The exasperation we felt was palpable and at each rejection, one of the lads made a dog-like whimpering noise. It seemed that no other sound could so aptly express our longings and frustrations, and the laughter, nervous at first, soon became uncontrollable.

Fifteen

On being recruited to the RAF, one becomes an aircraftsman, and after initial exams, a leading aircraftsman, and after further exams, a senior aircraftsman. I passed all my exams first time: the incentives were an increase in pay, a posting abroad, and no further study. But even these advantages did nothing to overcome the culture of anti-revision, and anybody who glanced at a notebook outside the classroom was branded a swot; the only time I could revise was in the lavatory!

After a short leave we were posted to Northern Ireland. I left home on a hot day dressed in full kit and had first to travel by Underground and then by train. On the ferry from Heysham to Belfast I slept on the deck, not realising how cold it could be on the Irish Sea. I awoke in the early hours of the morning, rain-damp and frozen with the cold. I tried to get below deck, but a carpet of sleeping airmen made it impossible. No wonder it was commonly referred to as "the cattle boat". We arrived at the camp in drizzling rain with kitbags on tired shoulders.

We were looking forward to a nice warm billet, but our accommodation had not been used since the war. So, first we queued for brooms, then we swept the huts, then we queued for our beds, then we assembled them. It was several weeks before we got warm water or heating, and there never was any NAAFI or recreational facilities. At first the food rations never kept pace with the new arrivals, so when the duty officer came around after dinner and asked, "Any complaints?" he got plenty.

But our lives were easier in other ways; there was no bullshit, no parades, and no kit inspections. On one occasion this liberal regime was shamelessly exploited. We were marching along a country road and saw a number of soldiers marching towards us. Their discipline had been stern, their conduct was immaculate, and their timing superb. On a suggestion by one of our lads we purposely disordered ourselves and broke step — just to flout our freedom.

In addition to working as radar operators we were to do guard duties. I was incredulous on being told that we were to patrol the perimeter fence with pick-axe handles and that, should we spot anybody trying to break in, one of us was to fetch the duty officer, who would then appear with a Sten gun. What the remaining aircraftsman was supposed to do in the meantime wasn't made clear.

This "Dad's army" procedure didn't last long, and within a few weeks we were all issued with Sten guns, and later still, floodlighting was installed to illuminate the perimeter fence. At the time, however, none of this seemed necessary, for the only hostilities were between the IRA and the RUC.

We were stationed near a tiny village called Ballyhornan, which was seven miles south of Downpatrick, and thirty miles south of Belfast. The bus service was so infrequent that we left the camp only if we had leave or a twenty-four-hour pass. To pass the time we would play poker, pontoon, three-card brag, Monopoly or Cluedo. I do not think any of us knew what "the troubles" were about, and politics was never discussed.

On the firing range, my Lee-Enfield rifle kicked like a mule, and the noise, so close to my ear, deafened me for several minutes. It was a disappointing experience, and my shoulder ached for some days afterwards. I obeyed, however, the written instructions to the letter and qualified as a marksman. Wearing both my marksman's and senior aircraftsman's badge made me feel very proud indeed.

Before commencing our patrols, we were issued with Sten guns, but my hands would get so cold that I carried mine slung over my shoulder. My hands had always been sensitive to the cold, they didn't go numb, like my feet, they went painful — it was as though the nails were being pulled off with pliers. Years later I realised I probably suffered from Raynaud's disease.

Instead of going out in twos, we unofficially agreed to do our guard duties alone, thus reducing them from four to two hours. On one particular night I heard footsteps approaching from the other side of the wire. "Halt, who goes there?" I cried. All was silent, and then I heard them again. I cocked my gun and repeated my challenge. Silence — then a cough — I began to sweat. Then, peering into the mist, I could just make out — a sheep! I did not then know that sheep coughed, but those did, frequently. It must have been all that cold night air.

I suppose where there are guns there will be accidents and we had our share. One lad, not long back from Korea, and possibly a little jumpy, shot a farmer's cow. Another lad let his Sten gun off by mistake and two bullets ricocheted off a wall and only grazed his face — how lucky was that! Then there were the two lads pretending to have a shootout, but with rifles instead of pistols — we had no pistols. One of the lads must have had a bullet "up the spout", for the rifle went off — and the bullet blew a hole in the ground between the other lad's feet!

Even I was not immune from the mistakes of others. One evening as I was letting a dog-handler through a gate, his dog sank its jaws into my calf. Once the vice-like grip was released, I started my tour of the perimeter fence — limping. The dog was put on a long chain, and whenever I limped past, he would bark and rush forward, straining at his leash, perhaps after tasting my blood he wanted more — I cocked my Sten gun just in case.

The next day, the dog handler thanked me for not reporting this matter; the dog should have been muzzled. Looking back, I am shocked at how accepting I was in those days. It would never have occurred to me to complain. I just accepted everything that happened without question. Even when I ceased to qualify as a marksman, it never occurred to me that my deteriorating eyesight was responsible. Although I would not let anyone take liberties with me on a personal level, anything else that happened I accepted without complaint — or thought. Was this typical of my generation? Nowadays, it seems individuals are far more self-aware, and are more inclined to question events and to challenge authority.

Sixteen

"Let's go to Belfast," said a friend one evening, "we can go by taxi." As I was incubating a rather aggressive cold, I was reluctant, but my friends talked me round, "A good drink will do you good." So off we went. My doubts about the wisdom of this decision occurred soon after we entered the first public house. "What's in all those pretty little bottles?" asked one friend, pointing to the liqueurs on the shelf. My friends were soon to find that curiosity is a dangerous instinct — I stuck to beer.

The ride back to our camp soon became a nightmare — "Open the window, open the window!" shouted the cabbie to my friend who was sitting beside him. My friend did as he was asked, then spewed out of the window and down the outside of the cab. My other friend, sitting beside me, looked dreadful; suddenly he leaned over in my direction and I raised my arm just in time to preventing him falling across me, at the same time I slid away in my seat and his vomit landed between us. By the time we reached our destination the taxi driver was raving mad, and when I discovered I didn't have enough money in my wallet to cover the fare, I wanted to die. I had to rifle the pockets of my comatose friends.

Seventeen

"How would you like to visit Dublin?" It was a question posed by the corporal in charge of our hut. He also suggested we might buy a few things "duty free". So off we went. I bought a wristwatch, and the corporal bought several packets of nylons and some lighters. On the train coming back the corporal stuffed his purchases into the pockets of his camel-haired overcoat, the coat was then flung onto the luggage rack. One item, however, had not been put in the overcoat — a table lighter — that was put in a holdall. My wristwatch was being worn around my ankle.

When the customs officer came around and asked if we had anything to declare, the corporal seized the initiative, "We have only the permitted cigarettes and wine — oh, and a table lighter."

"A table lighter! I'm sorry, sir, but you will have to pay duty on that," said the customs officer.

The corporal looked outraged. "Duty! Damn! I wouldn't have bought the bloody thing had I known." He kicked up such a fuss that I wasn't even asked if I had anything to declare.

A couple of years later, I went on holiday to Spain and while I was there, I bought a strap for my wristwatch. Going through customs, I had nothing to declare. "Would you take off your watch, sir?"

I explained that I had bought only the strap in Spain.

"And where did you buy the watch?"

"In Southern Ireland." Had I paid duty? "Yes."

"What colour was the form you signed?"

"I don't remember, buff, I think," (hoping that "buff" could be any colour from brown to yellow). My luggage was then thoroughly inspected; even down to unrolling my socks, examining my Brylcreem jar, and taking the lid off my shoe polish. Eventually, my watch was returned, and I was free to go.

Eighteen

Belfast was a favourite venue for a twenty-four-hour pass, and I would arrive early, book into a Salvation Army hostel and then go drinking and dancing. But on one wet Saturday afternoon I visited the central library and I came across a very old book on Irish humour — I mean, very, very old. It was falling apart and its pages were yellowing with age. Various items amused me, but there was one piece in particular that captured my attention:

A Drinker's Toast

Here's to all good fellows
In this world and the next
I drink to you this toast tonight
Good fellowship is my text

Not the fellow who takes your hand
In the idling hour, you know
Not the fellow who pats your back
As long as the drinks flow

But the fellow who speaks a kindly word
When the whole world's running low
The fellow who grips your hand like Hell
And tells you life's a song

What if we know the fellow lies
What if he knows it too
There are times in life when the friend that lies
Is the only friend that's true

So cavil and rant you prudes that will
On the evils of beer and gin
But sometimes the real true things we feel
Leak out when the drink leaks in

A fool is a fool, and a cad is a cad
Whichever God made him to be
But a man that's a man, won't forget he's a man
When out on a terrible spree

So drink this toast to your hearts tonight
From a heart, to a heart, let it run
For here's to good fellowship all over the world
Good cheer, good health and good luck, everyone.

After the dance I found the hostel closed; this was the second
time I had been locked out. The first time I had spent a
terribly cold night on the top deck of a bus. Not wanting to
repeat this experience, I tried to wake my friend by throwing
stones at a window next to his bed and had just given up
when a passing stranger suggested I should try the army

barracks down the road. On explaining my plight, I was allowed to sleep in the guardroom and at 5 a.m. I was given a cup of tea and told to leave before the duty officer came around.

Nineteen

I had some good friends in the RAF, and I went to Edinburgh with one, and to Newton-le-Willows, Lancashire, with another. I never went home. London was too far. So, when my mates suggested we buy an old banger to tour southern Ireland, I was enthusiastic, and when the car appeared, I was astonished. It was decorated all over with painted slogans: "S/Board" appeared on one mudguard, and "Port" on the other; "Six-Five-Special" was written above the windscreen, "C'est une voiture d'amour" ran along the bonnet, and on the back of the car was "Don't laugh, madam, your daughter might be in here."

The car was ancient and dramatically unroadworthy, it had poor steering and a broken silencer. There was not room enough inside the car for the four of us and our luggage, so we tied a kitbag to the front bumper. When we arrived at the border crossing, the customs officer threw up his hands in despair, then laughed and waved us through.

It was in the toilet of a Dublin pub that I saw a memorable piece of graffiti, "Pull the chain and in a jiffy, all your efforts in the Liffey". Perhaps it is only memorable because at first, I was puzzled, and then I got it. Wasn't the Liffey an Irish river? Could the river run alongside this pub? It was, and it did. Dublin reminded me of a poem written to Greenwich Village, (New York) "where life went to a gentler pace and dreams and dreamers found a place." Galway was quiet and beautiful.

On one occasion, our corporal would regale us with poetry. I was particularly impressed by a poem called *"The Yellow Dog"*. He said it was by Robert Service. I eventually went through the complete works of Robert Service — he of the Yukon — but found no "Yellow Dog"; was it by some other Robert Service — or did the corporal write it himself? The corporal had a rich, sonorous voice, and I loved the sound of the words.

The Yellow Dog

One pearly day of early May I strolled upon the sand
And so saw half a mile away, a man with gun in hand

A dog was answering to his call, so slow they sought to creep
Upon a dozen ducks, so still, they seemed to be asleep

When like a flash, the dog dashed out, the ducks flushed out in flight
The fellow gave a savage shout, and cursed with all his might

And so I stood somewhat amazed and gazed with eyes agog
In an angry rage, his gun he raised, he blazed and shot the dog

You know how a dog can cry in pain, its blood soaked in the sand
And yet it turned to him again and tried to lick his hand

What could I do, what could I say, t'was such a lonely place
Tongue-tied I saw him stride away, I never saw his face

I should have bawled the blighter out, a yellow dog he slew
But worse he proved beyond a doubt, that I am yellow too

It was explained that a gun dog that could not be trained, would invariably be shot.

The corporal said he was a friend of Robert Service and he would ask him to write a poem about any subject we cared to choose. At the time there was a popular song about a boxer, which went like this: "It was Tiger Wilson versus Kid McCoy in the summer of 93." And the refrain was: "Come on Kid, Come on Kid. Hit him with a left and a right. Come on Kid. Come on Kid. But how were they to know it was the kid's last fight."

I suggested a poem should be written about a boxer who, when successful, had lots of hangers-on, but when down-and-out, all his friends rejected him. The corporal did not think much of this, but the idea would not leave me alone, so I wrote the poem myself. It came to me, a verse at a time, over some weeks, or was it months? I didn't finish it until I was demobbed.

The Fall of the Champ

The bar door opened and in he reeled
The man they would all disclaim
A drunken tramp who was once a champ
A champ of the boxing game

In the ring he once was a king
His kingdom he shared with his followers
He treated them all, the big, and the small
And always had something for borrowers

Now here they all were, gold lighters and fur
The crowd he had treated so well
But now he was down, he received but a frown
And some would have seen him in hell

"Can you spare a drink?" he said to the mink
"For the guy you once promised to wed?"
But she picked up her glass and laughed at a joke
As though his words were unsaid

"How about you?" he said to the few
Who were joking at his expense
"Have you nothing to offer a man you once knew
Perhaps some small recompense?"

"Oh! Here's a drink" said the girl in the mink
"A big one so you won't grieve
I'm tired of your drunken drawl
So take your drink and leave"

He took the full bottle of Scotch to the door
Then turned for all to see
The cork he withdrew and spat to the floor
And said "Friends, listen to me

"I know I'm a tramp and a drunken sot
But I wish to propose a toast
A toast to the trollop I nearly got
Gentlemen, to my host"

He downed the drink in one go
Staggered and fell to the floor
His body had met its last foe
And his heart wouldn't beat any more

But his pitiful form caused no one to mourn
His life had all been in vain
For his death brought not grief, only relief
And his "friends" felt not even shame

That was the first creative writing I had attempted outside school and it came as a bit of a revelation. I had never experienced the creative process before, but was to realise that if you really want to say something, then your subconscious will find a way of expressing it — it may not be good, but it gets said.

I well remember my last dance in Belfast. In those days, Irishmen were very slow when it came to the fair sex and I was pretty slow myself. Then I saw this beautiful, sexy girl, dancing by herself on the far side of the dance floor. She was dancing in a sensual, uninhibited way, and I could scarcely

71

believe she was on her own — where was her boyfriend? Eventually, on overcoming my shyness, with a little alcohol, I walked to the other end of the dance floor and danced with her.

After taking this girl to a lonely spot near her home we indulged in some heavy petting. It was all so natural, and I clearly remember the thrill of her lithe young body as we embraced virtually naked, but at the very last moment she cautioned against full sex, but begged me to see her again. I made a date for the following Saturday. It was a date I knew I could never keep — it was my demob day. For the next few days I was distraught. I wanted so very much to see her again, but where could I stay? I thought of all possibilities, but nothing was practical.

We had agreed to meet in Belfast outside a baker's shop at four o'clock in the afternoon. I arrived, in full kit, at eleven o'clock in the morning — but I had written a letter. I gave the letter to one of the women working in the baker's and explained that I had arranged to meet a young woman at four that afternoon, but had received a sudden posting. The shop assistants thought this was terribly romantic, and I left the shop with damp eyes. In the letter I had written of my predicament and anguish, but left no forwarding address — what would have been the point? In those days, Belfast seemed so very far from London.

Twenty

I had enjoyed the company of the lads I was stationed with. Am I wrong, or are the Northerners emotionally warmer than us Southerners? If I am right, I suspect it's because they've had tougher lives. Is there not a quotation: "Men are made in adversity: monsters in prosperity"? The only occasion I nearly came to blows was when a Scottish lad caught a hare and put it in a cage, saying that it would be ready for the pot as soon as his leave came up. I told him he would first have to make me ready for the pot because I intended to release it. Our mutual friends cooled the situation, and after a couple of hours the hare was released.

On being demobbed, June 1956, I went back home to live with my parents and young brother. Nothing much had changed: my father was still contributing to the wealth of his bookie and publican, and my mother was still complaining about my father. I hadn't changed very much either, and one day my father gave me a "hot tip". He had attended a greyhound meeting the night before, where, in the bar, he had met two men who had given him a dog to bet on. The dog won, and my father was asked if he betted on the horses — is the Pope a Catholic? He was then given the names of two likely winners.

The first horse won, so I decided to "make a killing" and bet heavily on the second — it came in nowhere. Undaunted, I backed it next time out — it came in nowhere. Once more I bet on it; once more it lost. It was a good two-year-old, but as far as I am aware it never won anything as a three-year-old. It did, however, teach me a lesson — betting is a mug's game. It is a lesson my father never learnt.

***

I thought a holiday would be a good idea, but where to go, and who with? All my old mates had gone their separate ways so there seemed no alternative but to go somewhere on my own. I chose a hotel on the Isle of Wight, it was rather like a holiday camp and I entered several competitions — table tennis, golf, darts, snooker — and won some prizes.

On the last night, some newly acquired friends urged me to buy a bingo ticket. I had never played before — and I have never played since — but the one ticket I bought won me the jackpot and with the extra money I decided to stay on the island a day or two longer. I wanted to walk around the coast.

The following day was warm and sunny, and I made good progress along the beach until confronted by a cliff that jutted out to sea. On clambering up the cliff, I made my way through a great many blackberry bushes and worked my way along the top of the cliff until I saw another beach. Should I descend? The beach was only ten feet below, but the cliff was sheer. Could I get down? The only alternative was to go back, through all those scratchy blackberry bushes.

I threw my packed lunch over the cliff, eased myself over the edge and then dropped down. I soon discovered I was in a little cove and could proceed no further in either direction because of cliffs jutting out to sea, nor could I find any way of climbing back up the slippery clay cliff. But I was not worried. I had plenty of time. I would eat my sandwiches and wait for the tide to retreat.

I soon realised the tide was advancing and advancing fast. I was alarmed! How far would the tide come in? Could I wade around the cliff to the next beach? How far *was* the next beach? I put my half-eaten sandwich to one side and cautiously advanced into the sea, but the swell hit the cliff with such violent wallops that I decided to go no further. Should I try and swim? I was not a strong swimmer.

The main thing was not to panic — think! I then spotted a piece of driftwood. It was black, about five feet long and six inches square; one end was circumscribed with white lines, the other end had a sharp point — it looked as if it had been snapped off from a pier or jetty. Inspiration; I picked up the wood and drove the sharp end into the clay cliff, withdrew it, made another hole higher up, then another, and another — those niches enabled me to clamber up.

This was a very tiny adventure, insignificant compared to an Everest climb, or an ocean trip in a tiny boat, but then, all experience is relative. My life has been very small scale, my molehills mountains. Perhaps I exaggerated the danger. Perhaps I am lucky to be alive. I will never know, but then, every life has its little dramas.

Twenty-One

Having completed *The Fall of the Champ*, I felt the need to write some more. I sometimes chose verse, finding it easier to write than prose, for my grammar was pretty awful. Most of those scribblings were later destroyed, for I was embarrassed by their naïvety, sentimentality and foolishness, but I did keep some poems. Perhaps "poems" is too grand a description; perhaps doggerel would be more accurate. My only excuse for presenting them here is that they indicate a past need for self-expression, and betray a youth influenced by melodrama.

The Decision

He accepted the duel from a better man
Knowing full well he must lose
But she was watching and listening
So what other path could he choose?

The choice of weapons was his to name
But he was unskilled in all
"Pistols," he said, in a voice that was low
For he knew his chances were small

Now the day of the duel had arrived
And his face was drawn and white
He handled the gun with fear
His fingers they trembled in fright

"Bang"— now it was all over
No more had he to dread
For his foe was reeling painfully
And soon he would be dead

Much was the exclamation!
For they had not began to pace
Before his fumbling fingers
Brought him such wretched disgrace

But now his beloved came running
And caused his heart to beat
But she stopped aghast at the body
That was writhing at her feet

Over his body she bent
And the tears, how they did flow
As she cried "Oh my darling!"
In a voice that was very low

The trembling man did stare
His eyes seared by the sight
And glad was he to have made
Such cunning use of his fright

Burning Passion

What a story they could tell
What a story, what a Hell
How one day at Devil's Dyke
Riding round upon a bike
Never for one moment knowing
That the grass above was glowing

Fire was spreading ever quicker
And the smoke was getting thicker
Whilst those two on tandem gliding
Sometimes bumping, sometimes sliding
Giving shrieks of pure delight
Blissfully innocent of their plight.

The smoke descending like a cloud
Was soon to settle as a shroud
All too late they saw the danger
Terror making each a stranger
Each pushed forth in wild endeavour
Each fell down at end of tether

Alone they lay, slowly dying
Neither for the other crying
Which only goes to show, I guess
That when confronted by distress
We cannot tell until too late
How each will cope with bitter fate

Night Cares

In the dead of night
Are you ever in fright
Scared, and all alone?

With no one to kiss you
And no one to miss you
And no one to telephone?

Do you know what it's like in bed to lie
Thinking it may be better to die
With a choked off snuffle and groan?

Then think of others in similar state
Stop feeling sorry and master your fate
And prove to the world you have grown

Divinity Affinity

My God, He likes to take my hand
Though why I do not know

He makes me feel more confident
And so I grow and grow

Without Him, I'm a poor blind thing
Feeling all at sea

But with Him, I am ten feet tall
And He is ten foot three

From time to time I helped my father out with a job. It might have been painting, papering a ceiling, laying a felt roof, or taking out a fireplace. On such occasions my father's words came back to me, "You don't want to get into my game, son, it's too hard." It was hard, and tiring, and I could well understand my father's thirst for beer. I also felt sympathy for all such men of toil. I can't remember when I wrote the following poem, but it was reminiscent of another kind of life.

Just Another Saturday

Just another Saturday
A play on the BBC
I'd seen it all before somewhere
It was a part of me

The senseless violence, and the booze
To prove oneself a man
"I am a rough tough kiddie
Hurt me if you can."

And yet within that concrete jungle
Rough humour and the banter brought
Release from torpor and despair
And manly qualities were wrought

Together men in rough delight
Would drink and while away the night
And in the morning tired and grey
They'd face like lions another day

Twenty-Two

On completing the final year of my apprenticeship, I was to find that unless one was in the National Graphic Society, jobs in my trade were scarce, so scarce in fact that I decided to become a salesman. The training was excellent. We had an American manager who gave demonstrations that were truly inspirational, and within a few days I was part of a team and on the road.

There were usually six of us in the back of the van and another beside the driver — a position reserved for the best salesman of the previous week. We would be laughing and joking, attempting to keep our spirits high. Perhaps "Larry McCann — the give-away man" would be singing about the prospects of chewing gum losing its flavour, if left on the bedpost overnight.

The job attracted all types from students to ex-convicts, and on reaching our destination we would be dropped off, one by one, like paratroopers bailing out into unknown territory. Sometimes we worked on semi-detached houses with large front gardens and steps up to the front door — I found such property exhausting and unprofitable. I much preferred a friendly-looking close, with small gardens and no steps.

One cannot make a sale without getting into a house. One may achieve this by seeking "assistance with a survey", or by hinting that it could be advantageous, "I suppose you have seen the TV adverts?" Above all, one must create a good impression, remember the training — *"before selling the cleaner, sell yourself — a big smile is a good start."*

"Good afternoon, madame. Now I know you must be awfully busy, but could you possibly spare a couple of minutes for pre-market research?" The woman appears suspicious, but having seen I have only a clipboard in my hand and apparently nothing to sell, she invites me in. I then dash back to where I left my box and join the woman in the living room. After the initial shock, the woman likes the machine, but I cannot sell to her alone. I need her husband's signature on the contract. I arrange to return in the evening.

"Good evening, sir." I recall the training: *"Once inside you must have the householder's undivided attention. If the television is on, you switch it off, if they have visitors, make an appointment to return some other time."* On this occasion, the only instruction I needed to apply was: *"Always keep the husband and wife in front of you. You do not want one or the other signalling behind your back."*

Before opening the box, I look around the room. "This is a lovely room; it's not easy to find a good decorator nowadays."

"I know it isn't," says the husband, "that's why I do all my own"

"You did it yourself? Well you made a good job of it." I look around the room — is there anything else I can praise, a painting, a piece of carpentry, children? "Oh! A piano, you don't see many of those nowadays. Who plays?"

"Oh, I do, but I'm not very good," says the wife.

"Well, I wish I could, if only a little." I remark truthfully.

I take the cleaner out of the box with a flourish. "Well, what do you think of that!" I deftly swivel the machine on its castors and the chrome top gleams brightly.

"Oh, it's beautiful!" exclaims the wife.

I then proceed to give a good demo' while remembering my training: *"Give a good demonstration, get the head of the cleaner into those inaccessible places; produce dirt, lots of dirt."* On removing the dust bag from the machine, I upturn it onto the clean carpet and give it a good shake. I produce a nice circle of dust. The training says: *"Always look surprised when the dirt is produced."*

"Well, what do you think of that!" On this occasion, I am surprised, not by how *much* dirt I have produced, but by how *little*. Sometimes you can produce dirt that is truly amazing, and the householder doesn't bat an eyelid. This time, I am lucky.

"Oh dear! And I vacuumed only yesterday!" exclaims the wife. Cleanliness is obviously in the eye of the beholder.

The husband laughs and makes a joke at his wife's expense.

"Now don't blame your wife, sir. You, being a tradesman know the value of good tools and if your wife hasn't got the best, she can't do the best — can she?" *"It is important to seek agreement."* I look at his body language— is he nodding his head?

"Now if this was for sale in the shops, how much do you think it would cost?" The answer to this question can make or break a sale, therefore, since removing the cleaner from its box, I have been extolling its virtues against "those inferior machines in the shops that sell for £40."

"Oh, I don't know, at least £50," answers the wife. Since my machine costs only £30, I feel rather confident.

"You are very close — we expect it to retail at £45. Now I'm going to ask you a silly question. Do you like the machine?" She nods her head.

"Of course you do. What women wouldn't?" I then look at the husband, "Would you like your wife to have it, sir?" He can hardly say no — the sales technique is insidiously psychological. "Well, at my own discretion, I can let a machine go to a deserving couple..." They then commit themselves, thinking it might be a promotional offer, free, or at least a bargain — and at £30 it would seem a bargain.

It is then just a matter of getting a signature on the contract. "You haven't got the deposit? That's a pity." You start to pack the machine. "How much are you short? I'll tell you what, give me what you have and I'll put in the rest until your pay day."

"Always be ready to demolish any excuse: 'You can't afford the weekly payments? Do you smoke, drink...?'"

On occasions, I had sworn that a vacuum cleaner was not in the box. "Of course it's not a vacuum cleaner." I get inside the house. "It's a vacuum cleaner! You said it wasn't a vacuum cleaner"

I look sad, dejected, "Five years of research has gone into this and all you can say is, 'It's a vacuum cleaner.' It's a multi-purpose machine that not only cleans carpets, but also shampoos them; not only that, but you can also use it to dry your hair or spray paint — and all you can say is, 'It's a vacuum cleaner.' You say this with expansive good humour.

The householder knows you're being a bit cheeky, but he may also have a sneaking admiration for your audacity — and perhaps the additional tools *might* do what I say.

I made some remarkable sales. Once I gave a demonstration to a father and his two grown-up sons. "Boy, you're a great salesman," said one of the sons afterwards. "My father threw a vacuum cleaner salesman out of the house just a couple of weeks ago and now he has just bought a cleaner from you!"

On another occasion I sold to a couple who had no carpets, but they were obviously impressed by the cleaner. "Well," I said, "you won't be living like this forever, will you?" — and they bought it! And then there was the time the lads were amused to see me with a big radiogram — I had taken it in lieu of a deposit. One of the lads bought it from me immediately.

This may sound like fun, but then there were the bad times. The twitching curtains — the vigilantes who tracked your progress down the road — the buzzing telephones. Sometimes, doors were slammed in your face. Sometimes, after a demo', you would find the householder had a perfectly good vacuum cleaner. One could go for days without making a sale. And on a dark evening, how I would envy those people in their cosy little homes.

My morale would often depend on my afternoon's experience. After a bad time: "We get too many of you salesmen around here," my humour would become grimly sardonic, "Even the bloody cats look hostile!" On such a day, not even the juke box or the camaraderie of the team could lift my spirits. "Cheer up, Pete, it might never happen," says one of the lads.

"I'm afraid it already has," I reply, "I've answered the ad' — you know the one — the one that promises good pay and an interesting career for anyone with drive and initiative." We leave the café as Cliff Richard sings about his "living doll".

I was become increasingly demoralised. Why had I done this job for so long? Had I been convinced by the encouragement offered by the manager: "It takes guts and skill to be a good salesman." — "You are doing the customer a favour" — "If you can sell vacuum cleaners, you can sell anything." I suppose we managed to convince ourselves that some of this might be true, and then, once on the roller-coaster, it was difficult to get off. We were paid commission only: after a good week we felt buoyed up, optimistic; after a bad week we would strive to do better.

Feeling in need of a holiday, I went to the Isle of Portland in Dorset, and while I was there, I did some sketching. One of the things I sketched was an empty stone cottage, and as it did not appear to be locked, I decided I would return later and sleep in it. That evening, after a few drinks, I returned to the cottage only to find there were no floorboards! Undeterred, I tiptoed over the joists by the light of a match and found a few floorboards in the back kitchen. Everything was so dirty, but I had a newspaper with me and after spreading it on the floor, I slept well.

The following night I was in Weymouth, and I slept in what once had been a gun turret during the war. As it was made of concrete and was on top of a cliff, it was not the most hospitable of abodes, and during the night I woke up and did press-ups to get warm. On neither of these occasions did I have a sleeping bag — I must have been quite mad. So why did I do it? Well, money was quite tight, but I did, not out of necessity, but to see if I could survive.

I was so full of self-doubt; I had served a lousy apprenticeship and I hated selling vacuum cleaners, but what else could I do? How do the poor survive? This might sound foolish, but it is an indication of how insecure I felt at the time. What did the future hold? What was the worst that could happen? By sleeping rough I thought I was preparing for the worst that *might* happen.

On returning from holiday I gave in my notice — I felt I had sold my soul on the knocker.

Twenty-Three

Having always been naïve and romantic about the opposite sex I was incredulous when told that the girl who had placed the order was "on the game". The girl was very young, very pretty, and altogether lovely — not at all a stereotypical prostitute — there must be some mistake. I was still doubtful even when I saw the name and address, Miss Packy, Old Compton Street, Soho, W1.

I was working for a little jobbing printer's in Soho where I operated a platen press and produced promotional letters, leaflets, letter headings, and so on, and this young girl came in and ordered one hundred business cards. The manager gave the order to me, for he knew I did printing at home on my little Adana, and one hundred cards were hardly worth his trouble.

When I phoned the girl and told her the cards were ready, she asked if I could "be a darling" and bring them over. On approaching the girl's address, any doubts I'd had about her profession were soon clarified on seeing "The Model House" in big letters. I went through the doorway and saw a wide, iron, spiral staircase, and on climbing the stairs, I passed a voluptuous older woman coming down, she gave me a broad wink. When I reached the landing, I glanced at the doors, found the right number, knocked, and a maid took me through to a bedroom.

On another occasion, I printed some headed note-paper and envelopes for an address in Park Lane. It was an apartment block, and on giving the doorman the name of the person I wished to see, I thought he gave me a curious, searching look. I took the lift to the second floor, found the right door and rang the bell. A very old Chinese woman opened the door, and on entering the apartment, I was struck by its opulence: paintings and prints adorned the white-pilastered, flock-papered walls; deep pile rugs lay at my feet, and chandeliers and silver candlesticks provided the illumination.

I was greeted by an elderly, refined-looking man, dressed in a silk dressing gown. He invited me to be seated. I chose a chair, he a settee.

"Come and sit here," he patted the place beside him. "We can then go through the material together." I took the parcel over and sat down. "That's better," he said, putting his hand on my knee.

I shot up as though stung by a bee. "I'm married!" I blurted out. It might seem an absurd response in today's more sophisticated age, but I suppose you could say, it was a knee-jerk reaction.

Twenty-Four

After leaving the RAF I became increasingly critical of my parents' way of life. They were conservative by nature and subservient to the class system that prevailed. I doubt if either of them questioned the unfairness of it all, they just accepted it. I wish I could say their attitude was one of inverted snobbery, that they were proud to be working class, but no, they were neither proud nor resentful, they just accepted their lowly place in society without question. I suppose, to be fair, they felt there was very little that could be done to change matters.

I, on the other hand, began to question everything. I became increasingly critical of royalty, privilege and class; I wanted to see equal opportunity based upon ability and worth; I wanted to be accepted for what I was and might become. I can only suppose I was going through a rather giddy phase, in which I could see, or thought I could see, the infinite possibilities of life. I did not desire material things, but I did want to be better informed, cleverer, wittier. Alexander Pope was right: "A little knowledge is a dangerous thing."

Since leaving school I had become increasingly aware of my lack of education and poor background and had made some effort to improve both my speech and grammar. Nowadays, this must seem awfully snobbish, but in the 50s such things seemed important. My attempts to improve myself did not go unnoticed by my parents, and I was gently admonished or ridiculed for displaying what might seem middle class aspirations. My mother, on hearing me listening to classical music, said, "You're morbid, you are!"

My father would say, "People like us, don't do that."

However, the intoxication of a little learning went to my head, and some clever remarks culled from a book gave me inordinate confidence. Everyday conversation was so dull — why couldn't it be like the plays of Sheridan, Shaw, or Wilde? My rebellion, if that is not too strong a word for my political awakening, was strengthened after leaving the RAF. I read John Braine's *The Room at the Top,* saw *Look Back in Anger* at the cinema and was excited by the Angry Young Men Movement.

Change was in the air, and I wanted to be part of it. Perhaps my girlfriend also added to my longing for self-improvement. She worked as a secretary, had "O" levels and was no doubt more intelligent than I was. She introduced me to Shakespeare, Rupert Brooke and Robert Service. At that same time I read *Left Over Life to Kill* by Caitlin Thomas — this book increased my love of words — and Brendan Behan's *Borstal Boy* — such anger!

I met my girlfriend at a section-house police dance, but our favourite venue became the Hammersmith Palais de Danse. Ballroom dancing was popular in those days, and Joe Loss and his band were brilliant. My girlfriend lived with her mother, brother and some relations, in a big house in Brook

Green, and on occasions we would all gather together and sing Irish songs — I still love *Danny Boy.*

Our courtship was a long one, some three years, and rather innocent, for during that time we had never had full sex as she was a Catholic. However, she took a hand in relieving my frustration, so the only consequences were love bites. Those years were very good years. I enjoyed reading and writing and I always made great efforts to be entertaining.

So who was I? I was a working class lad made good — that's who I was. I had been in the RAF, had a lovely girlfriend, had proved I was strong and not without courage and was now earning a reasonably good wage — I felt equal to anyone. But this was conceit based upon wish fulfilment; it was arrogance, heading for a fall!

Twenty-Five

After getting the engagement ring from Hatton Gardens and a dispensation from the Church — pledging that any children we might conceive would be brought up as good Catholics — we had a church wedding in March 1961. This was followed by a big reception that was paid for by my mother-in-law. She worked as a supervisor/machinist in the rag trade so paying for the wedding and reception couldn't have been easy. Now, I can scarcely believe how I accepted all this with so little thought or appreciation.

After the wedding at Brook Green's Catholic church we bought a house near Strand on the Green, Chiswick. Houses were so much cheaper in those days, and the one we bought was cheap because it was hardly habitable. It had been sold by a man who had emigrated to Australia, and he had taken everything which might conceivably have been of some use, including all the electric light fittings — and the kitchen sink! The house needed redecorating throughout, and half the floor in the front room needed replacing because of dry rot.

We borrowed the deposit for the house from my wife's relatives, and I soon found a nearer, better-paid job, in Acton. This new place of work had another machine minder named Cyril. I was to find that Cyril took an instant dislike to me. I don't know why. Could it have been because I was to operate the bigger machine, and would therefore earn the higher wage? Did he feel that he should have been put in charge of it? Or was it because he did some part-time script writing for the BBC and this made him feel superior in some way? Whatever the reason, apart from making the odd supercilious remark, he completely ignored me.

I suppose it must sound odd that you can work in the same room with someone and not talk, but the noise of the machinery made conversation almost impossible, so it wasn't difficult. A compositor/manager worked on the floor above; he was an old man with a nervous, irritable disposition, always critical and never satisfied. He was assisted by a young trainee compositor; this trainee was good friends with Cyril, and they would take lunch together. I felt excluded and alone.

I suppose common sense should have prompted me to leave that job, but non-union jobs were scarce, and my skills and experience were limited. There was also the difficulty of applying for jobs. I had no access to a telephone, and my pay would have been deducted for any time I might take off — I never did take time off, I was too conscientious — I just soldiered on.

I can only imagine that my personality must have split during this period of my life; I was able to function at a practical level, I held down my job, and in company I could always "act the part," but the strain on my mental and emotional resources was huge. It seemed my life had changed from the carefree to careworn. I was working on the house obsessively, and the problems at work, and our debts, all took their toll.

I became single minded, and was driven by a deep sense of insecurity. I concentrated on the house and my job and regarded everything else as peripheral — even my marriage. My wife and I took elaborate precautions not to have children because of our debts — a mortgage and a loan from in-laws — consequently our sex life was far from satisfactory, it lacked spontaneity.

In my blinkered state, I resented anything that might make demands on my diminishing energy. One day, a man from an organisation called, "The Foresters" knocked on our door. We were told that we had been "recommended" by friends, but we could not be told who those friends were. After playing some ludicrous record on a portable record player, the man tried to sell us life insurance — to insure that, should one of us die, the other would have no financial worries.

I felt under pressure and was against committing myself to further expense without adequate consideration, but my wife thought it a good idea, so I signed the contract — I lacked the mental resources to resist. I had become a passive automaton. Good grief, I was so dispirited and distraught that I would have bought an elixir from a sick man.

Why, oh why, did I not seek help! Why didn't I share my worries? Pride, I suppose, and habit; I had never shared my anxieties with anyone, I had learned to keep my thoughts, doubts and fears, to myself — a big mistake.

Twenty-Six

I was surprised to learn that the manager/compositor was retiring! God knows what age he was. He looked much older than sixty-five, and with his wizened face, beak-nose and jutting jaw, he reminded me of Mr Punch. On his last day he arrived driving a brand new sports car — a convertible — and he was dressed in a blazer and slacks. It was the first time I had seen him looking happy and relaxed.

Had he fulfilled a lifetime's ambition, was he now about to recapture lost youth? Well, we all need our dreams and today I would warm to such a sight, but at the time I was full of resentment. This old bastard had never uttered a civil word to me, so when he came round to shake hands and say his good-byes, I deliberately turned my back on him.

The new manager, a Canadian, seemed a very decent chap; life at work would surely improve. However, within a few days of this new manager starting, Cyril made a sarcastic remark that I clearly heard. His remarks were usually just out of earshot and uttered for the benefit of the trainee alone. I cannot now remember what was said, but I flew into a rage and a fight ensued. The new manager broke it up and demanded to know what it was all about.

I started to explain, but it was the end of the working day, and I noticed my antagonist walking towards the exit door with a smirk on his face — perhaps he was looking at the remnants of the shirt he had torn from my back. I just had time to shout out "I'm going to have you!"

The next morning, I concealed myself in a garden of a house I knew Cyril would have to pass to get to work. As he came striding down the road I suddenly stepped out and challenged him. He didn't stop, but carried on.

"I don't believe in fighting," he said, in his superior tone.

"You're going to fight me," I replied. A couple of straight lefts to his face soon converted him.

He was very strong and wrestled me to the ground, but I ended up on top. I heard some women screaming at me to get off him, but he was holding my wrists in a grip of iron, which was just as well, for given half the chance I would have smashed his head against the kerbstone. The fight was broken up by a policeman, and as we were being questioned our manager turned up and smoothed matters over.

 Later in the day I was still seething with rage. Cyril was watching his machine, and between us there was a large stone table with a mallet on top. I wrestled with my conscience for some minutes: Wasn't Cyril to blame for my abysmal morale? Why should I not pick up the mallet and smash his head? But he had his back to me. Could I take such an unfair advantage? Also, he had not pressed charges, so he was not thoroughly bad. What about the police officer — would he get into trouble, if, after letting me go, I committed murder? The voice in my head was insistent, "Pick up the mallet!" The reasons for and against tormented me — why shouldn't I be judge, jury and executioner? How very, very narrow seemed that gap between the thinking and the doing! When I got home my wife thought I had been in an accident — my coat sleeve was covered in blood.

I can scarcely remember the following week I just functioned on autopilot. I seem to remember snapping at one point. I broke something and hit my wife, not deliberately — I just lashed out. I don't think I hurt her, but I must have scared her. The following day she asked for a trial separation. I was apathetic, "If you like — when?"

"Tomorrow," she said.

I shrugged, "OK." Just like that, as if she had suggested a picnic — but had she proposed a suicide pact, I feel sure I would have responded in much the same way.

I later attempted some kind or reconciliation. My wife was then living in a lodging house outside London. I adopted what I imagined was a strong, masterful role — well, it always worked for Clark Gable — I took her by the arm and said, "Come on, get your things together, you're checking out." Of course she wasn't. She got me on the other side of the door and locked it.

"It's no wonder she left you if you behave like that," said the landlady. Yes, indeed.

Twenty-Seven

During the period when our marriage was still holding together, my wife and I had joined the local Liberal Party. One of the members was an attractive older woman, and it was to her that I turned when my wife left me. Sonia was a divorcee; she had an antique business in Knightsbridge and a son at boarding school. I was alone and desperate; she was sympathetic, intelligent, and easy to talk to — I suppose under the circumstances an affair was inevitable.

This was the first intimate friendship I'd experienced outside marriage, and I was flattered that a sophisticated woman should find me attractive. When Sonia suggested we might go to the theatre, I insisted on paying my way. On a Saturday I would visit her house in Chiswick with a bottle of Dimple's whiskey. Sonia seemed to favour this brand because its squat size was able to fit inside her sideboard. On the following Sunday morning against a background of classical music, we would read and discuss articles in the broadsheets.

Our affair never seemed quite real to me, I felt it was a hothouse relationship that would never survive the cold air of reality. Sonia had strict rules: I could stay over on a Saturday but no other day, as she was mindful about what her neighbours might infer. I understood Sonia's guarded behaviour, she had to consider her reputation, and in those days, society was not so permissive.

But one Sunday I did stay over and then had to leave the house at a very early hour, shoes in hand, so not to wake anyone. On my way home, the dawn chorus suddenly erupted. I had never heard this before and I was struck by the exhilarating drama of it all. It seemed as if all those birds were singing for my benefit alone.

Sonia was not flamboyant, but on one occasion she did surprise me — she tipped a bagful of sovereigns all over the bed before we made love on it! She also hinted at marriage, in a wistful sort of way, and then indicated that she was a silly woman for even thinking about it.

I was surprised. Even had I been free to marry, marriage to Sonia would have been unthinkable. She was above me in class and breeding and had both money and a profitable business — I would have felt like a ponce. In addition, the difference in our ages, some twelve years, would not have boded well for the future. No, this was not a serious relationship, but a digression, a refuge.

When Sonia introduced me to Margaret, Margaret told me in passing that her husband had been very critical of the film *The L Shaped Room.* I was shocked and incredulous because I had thought it a lovely film and so "of our time". I suppose the fact that I remember this so clearly is an indication of how opinionated I then was.

Margaret must have thought I was some kind of stud. She said she would like to know me better, that I should learn to drive and that she would pay for the lessons. She told me that her husband had left England to lecture in the United

States. I was confused, this was Sonia's friend — was Sonia a party to this? I turned down her offer.

During this period, I was still trying to mend bridges with my wife. This might appear incongruous, but it was my wife who had suggested the trial separation, and as far as I was concerned, that was all it was. I thought she was giving me time to come to my senses, to find my true self, and that soon we could make a fresh start. I could not believe we would not get back together again.

Eventually, my wife agreed to come back home to discuss matters. During our discussion my wife asked if I was seeing anybody else. I have always been too honest for my own good and like an idiot I said yes, I had been seeing Sonia? And had I slept with her? "Yes." Although this confession was impulsive, I was conscious at the very same time of an element of triumph, an implicit, "you may not have wanted me but somebody did".

Of course, after this there was no more discussion, she was adamant: we were finished. I had accepted the original break with a shrug of my shoulders, zombie-like, so my reaction on this occasion must have been startling. I became demented: I apologised, I begged, I raved with grief, I prostrated myself in agonies of regret. I wondered afterwards what she must have felt: pity, loathing, contempt — probably only relief. I knew she was seeing somebody else and now she could rid herself of me with a clear conscience.

After this I decided to visit my wife's mother. I knew I would not be welcome, so on my way I went to a pub and fortified myself with three double-whiskeys. How could I have been so stupid? I can scarcely now identify with such stupidity, but at the time my behaviour contained more than an element of self-dramatisation. Wasn't this the way a man was supposed to behave? Such behaviour was common in films and my father frequently used Dutch courage. The publican's wife was intrigued, but I refused to satisfy her curiosity.

My mother-in-law wouldn't let me into her house, but she told me that her daughter was no longer living there. No, she did not know where she was staying. I was then asked to leave. I so desperately needed to talk, but my mother-in-law was in no mood to listen. She then called out for her son Jim, who lived in the flat above.

Was she trying to intimidate me? I was in no mood to be intimidated, but nor was I feeling belligerent. I just wanted to talk, to apologise, to see if there was any hope, any way, that I could make amends. With this in mind I also called out for Jim. I then found myself engaging in an absurd duet with my mother-in-law, sometimes dissonant, sometimes in harmony. Jim didn't come down; I think his wife restrained him.

As all else had failed, I tried writing letters. Eventually, my wife's solicitors informed me that my letters had been destroyed, unread, and that if I attempted to see either my wife or her family again, a restraining order would be sought. That did the trick. I was gutted — and the bloody Beatles kept singing, "*She loves you, yeah, yeah, yeah.*"

Twenty-Eight

My wife, of course, did the sensible thing. she realised she had made a bad mistake, put it behind her and then carried on with the rest of her life. I should have done the same, but I was distraught and bereft. Sonia moved to Brighton, and I was left to brood and drink. It was not the careless, light-hearted drinking for social occasions, but the deliberate, despairing drinking of solitude, seeking oblivion.

I blamed myself for everything and I would sit night after night in a noisy, juke-box bar, trying to work out how I could have made such a mess of everything. It was like trying to solve some complex puzzle — I would recall incidents and conversations and would despair at my ineptitude. It was a very painful process, but I had to work out what had gone wrong, and why. I had to understand how I could have been such an idiot.

I wrote in my diary, "Hell is living with the realisation of one's past mistakes." I then wrote a poem:

Love Lost

A little boy plucked the fairest rose he ever saw
But wandering in a wood, he got lost
He became distressed
The rose's head he tore

Emerging from the wood, he sighed
And now he was a man
But on looking at the headless, thorny stalk
He cried

In spite of everything I still held down my job, and the new manager brought about some changes. A new, expensive printing machine was bought, a Heidelberg cylinder, and they put Cyril in charge of it. But Cyril couldn't cope; his experience had been on much smaller, slower machines. I was then put in charge of it, and Cyril was dismissed — a Pyrrhic victory? I felt no sense of triumph.

Cyril's replacement was a man who appeared always to be deep in thought, but he never had anything to say. His stolidity often got on my nerves. What with drinking heavily and having no real friends, especially of the female variety, I became a bit of an outsider.

Once this process starts, unless checked, it can only get worse; you begin to feel separated from the real world as if by an invisible barrier. You begin to feel like an alien, a singleton in a world of couples — and loneliness becomes a constant companion. You feel you may be an object of pity or suspicion and you avoid eye contact. You realise that you must appear aloof and anti-social, but cannot break through the restraint of self-consciousness.

I wrote a few poems that expressed something of what I felt at that time:

Self-Consciousness

Who are they out there?
I wonder what they're thinking
They make me feel like shrinking
I wish they would not stare

The brain's vain search for hidden slight
The ear that strains for whispered mockery

That man, I feel that he is sneering
Though why I do not know
Those two I think that they are jeering
I wish that they would go

The flushed face that belies indifference
The averted eyes that beg surrender

Anonymity

Today I went for a swim
I set off along anonymous streets
Past anonymous dwellings
Navigated flows of anonymous
traffic
And, after buying a ticket from an anonymous man
And swimming in an anonymous pool with anonymous people
I returned home
To an anonymous life

Hidebound

I'd like to kiss, cuddle and cavort
Without a thought
But being introspective
Not even a detective
Could see me do such a thing
Even in spring

Twenty-Nine

A little insight can go a long way. I used to suffer bouts of depression that were almost unendurable, but when I realised they had only a limited duration, they became easier to bear — like entering a tunnel and waiting for the light at the other end. On coming out of the tunnel, I would sometimes act a little out of character; this is one such instance:

On entering the pub, the depth of the bar surprised me and as I made my way to the counter at the far end, I observed the customers on either side of me. They were, for the most part, men of foreign origin and they were seated at small round tables. At the far end of the bar, in front the counter, sat two beautiful young girls. They were scantily dressed, and one of them was wearing a wide-brimmed, straw hat — no doubt they were taking time out from the Revue Bar next door.

You might ask what I doing in a pub like this, right in the middle of Soho. Well, the explanation is simple: I had been at a loose end, bored, restless, and sexually frustrated. I wanted to go somewhere new, somewhere exciting. What about Soho? Oh, I knew its reputation, a sleazy district full of clip joints and dodgy people, but having worked there, I felt confident of avoiding any trouble, and it would be a bit of an adventure.

Drinking alone usually made me introspective and subdued, but tonight I felt confident. I'd already had several beers, so I walked over to the girls' table, smiled and asked if I could buy them a drink; my eyes settled on the girl in the straw hat, she shook her head, but her friend said, "Yes." Then the girls conferred briefly, and the final answer was "No."

On finishing my drink, I went over to the girl's table, and in passing, whipped off the girls' hat. As I strode towards the exit, I heard the girl cry, "Oh no, not my hat, please!" but I carried on walking, aware that all eyes were upon me. Then having reached the door, I turned around and with a broad flourish spun the hat the full length of the bar. It sailed like a Frisbee, and the girl, still seated, stretched out her hand and caught it by the brim.

Whether the applause was for me, the girl, or for both of us, I shall never know, but the look of delight on the girl's face was gratification enough. Only later did it occur to me that this moment of madness could have turned out quite differently. There had been some tough-looking customers in that bar, and I was fortunate that nobody had intervened. I suppose the suddenness of the little drama halted any immediate intervention, and then the stylish dénouement defused the situation.

Thirty

Although I had removed from the house every last vestige of my wife, there were still too many unhappy memories. Sandie Shaw sang, *Always Something There To Remind Me,* and Peter and Gordon were singing about living in *A World Without Love* — and like Dusty Springfield, I just didn't know what to do with myself. The poignancy of those words was almost too much to bear. Noel Coward was so right about the potency of cheap music.

I was now drinking six nights a week, but it was only when I thought of buying whiskey so I could have a nip in the morning that I realised the danger of becoming an alcoholic. What a sad, contemptible sot I was becoming. I would have to change my life, and to do that I would have to make some radical decisions. Resolutions: I would go on holiday, and on my return, I would sell the house.

As soon as I got to Paris, my silly schoolboy conviction that "it is pointless to learn French when you know you will never go to France", came back to me. It was June 1965 and I had booked into a modest hotel. Money was tight but I would live frugally. Wine was incredibly cheap, and I would buy bread and cheese. Buying the bread was easy, but where to buy the cheese? I then found a shop that had cheeses of every shape and size, but they were all so big — then I saw a little one.

On paying for the cheese, the young girls in the shop giggled and gesticulated in consternation. What was the matter with these girls? I soon found out; the cheese was Parmesan, and try as I might, I could find no way of getting into it — it was like a tough rubber ball. I consoled myself with the bread and the wine, which I shared with some hippies on the Left Bank.

There were several magazines around at that time advising on cheap travel. One of these suggested that one could get a free meal by queuing up in the refectory of the Sorbonne University. I duly queued up, nobody questioned me, and I got my free meal. I felt rather guilty about it afterwards.

One evening I went to a café in the Pigalle district and got talking — in English — to some French guy. He began boasting of his strength and asked me if I knew how to arm-wrestle. I felt quite confident, but he was bigger and stronger and claimed as his prize a gossamer condom that he had spotted in my wallet — in exchange he gave me a French letter. It was like substituting a silk vest for a woollen one! I didn't mind, I had no prospect of using mine, whereas he immediately put his to good use with a girl in the bar.

A few days later I was on a train to Marseille, when a Frenchman offered me some baguette. In return I offered him my whiskey. It was a pleasant non-verbal exchange in which a feeling of good will was engendered. Then, on reaching Marseille, I spent a lazy afternoon sunning myself on a beach — it was a beach I was later to recognise in the film, *The French Connection*.

When I left the beach, I walked around the steep, narrow, cobbled streets. Where could I stay for the night? I felt distinctly ill at ease, for on every corner rough-looking characters loitered, and I felt I was attracting more than a passing interest. I felt very vulnerable. I took the next train to Cannes.

I arrived at Cannes late at night, left the station, turned right and walked along a deserted road. After a mile or more the road petered out, and I found myself walking through shrubbery. I was dismayed. Should I go back or could I find a clearing, somewhere to lie down? Suddenly I heard a noise, and it was getting louder; it sounded like some heavy animal was bursting through the undergrowth and was heading in my direction! I retraced my steps at top speed.

By now it was well past midnight and the railway station was closed. I kept on walking and eventually arrived at a beach. I sought shelter beside one of the boats on the shingle and was surprised to find some other vagrants there, one of whom assured me that the tide would not reach us.

The next night I slept in a deckchair. It was in a little garden opposite a casino. Two gendarmes woke me and asked to see my passport. I had visions of being dragged off to the local gendarmerie, or whatever the local cop shop is called, but the gendarmes were surprisingly courteous; they returned my passport and left me to get back to sleep.

On returning to England, I set about resolution two: the selling of the house. I felt the sooner I could sell the property, the sooner I would feel free. How naïve! Freedom is largely a state of mind and I was still suffering from a state of loss — like bereavement. Had my wife at that time contacted me from the other side of the world and said, "Come, I need

111

you", I would have gone, without question — like a Lorenz gosling pursuing emotional security.

The house was fully furnished and contained some good pieces of furniture, among which was a round, rosewood, folding-table (a wedding present), a mahogany, glass-fronted bookcase, which I had bought from a friend, and a heavy, hand-carved sideboard — all antiques. My state of mind was such that I could not be bothered with any of it; in fact, I thought it would be an added incentive for somebody to buy the house! When the buyers said they did not need it, I just said, "Well, get rid of it." Years later, on watching the "Antiques Road Show", I realised I had left behind a small fortune.

Thirty-One

A fresh start! The house had been sold, and I had found another job. I would be selling teaching-aids for children and would be visiting US army bases in Stuttgart, Germany.

I travelled by train with a number of young people and I was probably the oldest. It was only at the journey's end that I realised the job had been misrepresented. I could scarcely believe my stupidity. No wonder the interviewer had responded so encouragingly when I told him that my only selling experience had been selling vacuum cleaners — the new job was to sell encyclopaedias!

On arrival, we were given a brief tour of the camps — they were isolated, grim and depressing, and I could tell they had been "well-knocked". The young people previously recruited appeared dispirited, and I sensed they felt trapped and desperate. I had a return ticket in my wallet and I made it quite clear to the people in charge that I would be returning to England the following day.

The people in charge took this news surprisingly well; that evening they took me out drinking, and the next day they drove me to the railway station. At first I was puzzled by this courtesy, but I later suspected that they wanted to keep me away from the other recruits; that my departure might demoralise them — or was it feared that I was a newspaper reporter?

On returning to England, I went to Earl's Court Underground station. I was of the opinion that Earl's Court was an exciting bed-sit land and I was hoping to find accommodation there. Opposite the station was a pub with a pay phone, and from there I tried all the "to let", places that were being advertised in a nearby shop, but all in vain. I then bought an evening newspaper and found a cheap hotel in Highbury, North London. The hotel contained a motley collection of transients; mostly the unemployed and the unemployable, but I found a job as a printer.

It was another noisy machine shop in drab surroundings and artificial light — what was I doing with my life? I must get out of here! During my lunchtime I usually eat a sandwich and read a book, but not today: today, I would go out. The brilliant sunshine took me by surprise; everything seemed especially beautiful, in Technicolor — people — grass — trees — I walked around in a kind of daze. How much time had I left? I looked at my watch. The thought of having to return was causing my head to throb. I'd had this throbbing before, but nothing like this. I wondered whether a vein might burst. On returning to work, I gave in my notice.

Now, what was I to do? What *could* I do? The only knowledge I had, was of the printing trade; perhaps another printing job in another part of the country? I applied for two: one in Banbury, the other at Shoreham-by-Sea. I was offered both, but I accepted the latter thinking the sea air would do me good. Shoreham-by-Sea is a bit of a misnomer — Shoreham-by-Estuary would be more accurate, for I saw no sea, or sand, or promenade; it is, or was, a provincial backwater, pleasing to the eye, but deadening to the heart and soul.

At first, I lived with a family, but when the family sold their house and moved to Worthing, I moved to Brighton. Soon after this I was dismissed from my job. I'm not sure why, no reason was given, and I didn't ask. I was not too bothered. I had made no close friends, and there was an air of anxiety about the place; when the governor came around, some of the staff actually touched their forelocks.

***

On a pub-crawl, somewhere between Brighton and Hove, I came across a bar, or was it a private club? It didn't look like a public house. I went up the steps, opened the door and approached the counter. Almost immediately a woman came over and asked for a light, and as I ordered my drink, she ordered one as well. When the barmaid charged me for both drinks, I made it plain — I was paying for only one. The barmaid apologised and refunded the price of the woman's drink.

Suddenly, the woman became abusive and she walked to a table where some seafarers were sitting, she spoke to them and pointed in my direction. She was obviously encouraging them to do me over. I thought it best to act confidently and I raised my glass before them as if drinking a toast. I then coolly looked around the room, hoping to be thought a plain clothed policeman. On finishing my drink, I made my way unhurriedly towards the door, but once outside, I decided on a more hurried departure.

***

At the labour exchange I was asked what sort of work I would like. The interviewer was about my age, and I told him I quite liked the look of his job. He looked thoughtful, asked about my qualifications and then went off somewhere. When he came back it was business as usual. I knew without being told that without educational qualifications I stood no chance of getting such a job. I was grateful, however, that the interviewer had apparently seen me as a likely candidate.

As the weeks passed, my confidence waned, and after two months I began to doubt whether I was capable of doing anything useful at all. I told the labour exchange I was prepared to do any type of work, even labouring, but was told there was no such work available. When a woman from the DHSS visited my bed-sit, she was disparaging. She thought, on judging from my previous earnings and work history, that I could have done a lot better for myself.

I had been living in Brighton for some months, and during that time had joined an amateur dramatics group. We did *Inherit the Wind* — it was a lot of fun. I even had a girlfriend for a while. But all my acquaintances had benefited from a good middle class education and were enjoying the life-style that went with it: a good job, a car and a social background different from my own.

I was not at the time consciously seeking social mobility, and had I found myself among the working class I feel sure I would have embraced that life-style. After all, my background *was* working class: the poverty of my youth, the outside lavatory, the tin bath, the icicles *inside* the bedroom windows, my illiterate friends and a poor education — and yet, I didn't feel working class. I felt neither working class nor middle class — I felt an outsider.

However, Christmas was approaching, a time of parties and good cheer.

Thirty-Two

Now was the time to be decisive; I had thought about it several times before, the only problem was, how best to go about it. When I set out to do something, I like to do a good job. Jumping off a high building wouldn't do, as I couldn't bear the thought of my parents having to identify my mangled body. Would my parents blame themselves for my death? I hoped not, but if so, I would not choose to add to their pain with a messy suicide. I ruled out hanging for the same reason.

Pills *would* be the answer, if only I could rely on them, but I had read of individuals who, in using this method, had failed to do the job properly. Many of those failed attempts were, no doubt, "cries for help," but what about those who had survived only to find that they had irretrievably damaged their bodies? It might seem odd to worry about damaging your body when you are bent on suicide, but the thought of a damaged body frightened me. Suppose I woke up in hospital full of tubes and awaiting a liver or kidney transplant! No, I wanted a non-messy, guaranteed way out.

Gas! That was the answer. Gas would provide a foolproof, painless death, and I had read somewhere that the body takes on a rosy hue — I would look quite healthy. (I now think this assumption was quite wrong; it is carbon monoxide poisoning that creates a rosy hue — or am I still wrong?) I had no gas stove but I did have a gas fire. I put lots of coins in the gas meter and a rolled-up towel at the bottom of the door of my room. I then draped a blanket around the gas fire and over my body.

I was quite comfortable; I had a cushion under my head and the hissing gas was quite reassuring — not long now. However, it seemed to be taking ages, and although I was not in any particular hurry, I was worried I would not succeed. What could be the matter? I started taking very deep breaths, "Come on, Death, I am ready for you." And I drifted off, off, off. Suddenly, I heard a voice — it was very clear and authoritative.

It was a rebuke of such authority that I was shaken to my very core and I immediately turned off the gas. I then struggled with the blanket and tried to stand up, but on succeeding, I collapsed onto my bed. I lay there spread-eagled, fascinated by the room revolving around me — a carousel of bewilderment. After some minutes I staggered over to a large window, it would not open, but I then stood on a chair and managed to open a smaller one — I took in deep breaths — it was good to feel the cool night air in my lungs.

The following morning, I awoke in a state of trepidation. What the hell was wrong with me? I needed help. I got dressed and went to the nearest phone box. I dialled the operator. "Oh, hello, a friend of mine has tried to commit suicide, could you give me the number of the organisation that might be able to help him?" I could detect the concern in the operator's voice as she asked me to wait. Of course, she suspected whom the information was really for — it was implicit in my voice. The operator gave me the number of the Samaritans in central London. I phoned, and on receiving directions on how to get there, I took the next train to Victoria.

St. Stephen Walbrook is an old stone church, and on arrival I was directed to the crypt where some old ladies were busy making tea. From there I was led into a small room and greeted by a very young clergyman. On pouring out my sorrows, I became rather detached, and like a disinterested listener, I heard my grief-stricken voice echoing off the low, vaulted, ceiling.

Suddenly, the telephone rang. It was obviously the clergyman's girlfriend, and before my eyes he changed from a caring listener, to a relaxed boyfriend, and then back once more to the caring listener. He then gave me the telephone number of a man I could contact, should I need to talk to somebody in future.

I realised that this young clergyman had no real empathy with my situation. I didn't blame him; he was young and from a different background, and it occurred to me that he must have heard so many sad stories, many much worse than mine. My visit, however, was not wasted: my "detached voice" — my snivelling alter ego, had provoked in me such shame and contempt that I resolved to make a fresh start. On returning to my boarding house, everybody was talking about the gas!

I later found the cause of my failure: at the back of a gas fire there is a vent that allows all the fumes to go up the chimney — this must have been where much of the gas had gone. As for the "voice," I don't know how to explain it. I had even wondered about an angel, but I discounted the idea,

I could not imagine why any angel should think my life worth saving; and then the "voice" didn't sound feminine.

Since then I have learned from those that know, or think they know, claim that angels are masculine. However, as I now no longer believe in angels. Oh my God, an angel just dropped dead! I can only conclude that the "voice" popped out of my sub-conscious — I am sure that most of us have experienced a dream so startling, that we have woken up from a deep, deep sleep.

Thirty-Three

I saw the writing on the wall: computerised, photographic imaging, would soon replace hot-metal type, and offset lithography would soon replace letterpress. Lithography was proving to have many advantages over letterpress: it was cheaper, quicker and more versatile. I felt it was just a matter of time before letterpress became, if not obsolete, certainly obsolescent. I was thirty-one years of age; the sooner I looked for alternative work, the more likely I would succeed.

It was February 1966, and on looking through a newspaper I saw two possibilities: the Royal Air Force and the General Post Office — I applied to both. I found the test for the Post Office rather difficult — English and arithmetic — but I was offered the post of Clerical Assistant. The RAF multiple-answer paper was easy, even when not sure of the answers I could make intelligent guesses.

When the RAF examiner asked what trade I would like, I said lorry driving, thinking that this would not only be a useful skill to have, but would also offer the opportunity to travel and meet people. I was told there were no vacancies for lorry drivers, but as I had shown a marked aptitude for electronics, I would be suitable for the position of Ground Telecommunications Technician. I was flattered; during my

National Service, those guys were higher in the pecking order than radar operators.

The more I thought about it, the more doubtful I became; was the RAF wrong about my aptitude? After all, I had studied basic electronics during my National Service, so I was bound to know a little. On visiting the local library, I took out two books on basic telecommunications — all those equations — no thank you! I therefore accepted the offer from the Post Office.

My parents, on hearing about my new job, suggested I move in with them. At first, I hesitated, it seemed a step in the wrong direction. I valued my independence and to go back home would seem like defeat. But I soon realised it made a great deal of sense. My mother and younger brother would be glad of my company, and the rent would be affordable — the drop in my wage, or should I now say, salary, was to be considerable.

The London Telecommunications Region was situated in a high-rise office block overlooking the Thames. On entering, I was greeted by a smiling face, taken by lift to a higher floor, and was shown my desk and telephone. Now this might sound very over-the-top, but to me, this was fantastic. No noise, no depressing workshop, no grubby overalls — instead, I would be working in a bright, quiet, open office, dressed in a suit and treated with respect. What is more, I would be only working thirty-seven hours a week and would be entitled to three weeks holiday a year — it was like a dream.

My colleagues were friendly, and the work was easy. I had only to do some simple calculation on a slide rule and enter the results in a book. My only fear was the telephone; at first, whenever it rang, I was almost too scared to pick it up — we never had a phone at home.

The contrast between factory and office was scarcely believable. When I heard somebody saying that he still had twelve Whitley Days left, in addition to his holidays, I was baffled — what were these Whitley Days? It transpired they were days that could be taken off without having to produce a doctor's certificate — they were often used as additional annual leave! At a previous job my wage had been docked for being ten minutes late! This was a different world.

Thirty-Four

Circulars would regularly appear on my desk keeping me informed of new regulations, staff changes, etc., and when I read about a dingy sailing course at Burnham-on-Crouch, I decided to give it a go. It was something I would never have contemplated, or even heard about, had I not been in the civil service.

The course lasted five days, and there were five boats, each manned by a crew of four. The weather was so windy that sails had to be reefed; even so, four of the boats capsized, but not mine. I had never sailed before, and the contrast between running with the wind and tacking was dramatic — with the wind behind, all is calm and smooth, but turn into the wind, and a cold, heavy spray takes your breath away.

When I returned to the office, I was made aware of the civil service clerical examination. Passing it would bring promotion and a higher salary. I was advised to buy some previous copies of the exam from Her Majesty's Stationery Office. On examining past papers, I could see it was a very practical exam: English comprehension, précis, essays, letter writing and arithmetic.

I felt confident that, with some serious study, I should be able to pass the exam. To improve poor spelling, I made a list of the most commonly misspelt words and learned them by heart. I also went to night school. At the school I was asked to write an essay relevant to what one finds in a larder. I wrote about intensive farming, the abuse of nature and nature's imminent revenge. The tutor kept my essay till last, and when he returned it, he said it was very good and well within 'O' level standard. I was pleased, but also impatient; I was so desperate for a cigarette and a beer.

When I passed the civil service exam, I had the choice of which department to work for. I had found my life at Camelford House rather boring, so I chose the Department of Employment.

***

"What's the matter with you people, are you all zombies?" The telephone engineer was expressing his disgust at having been ignored. He had enquired about some telephone extensions, and we had all remained silent. Had he asked an individual, it would have been different, but he had addressed his questions to the section as a whole, and none of us felt obliged to respond. We had not ignored him out of discourtesy, but only because we were too busy — we did not want to be disturbed. We had no time to answer questions.

Perhaps I should have stayed with the Post Office; working on the "benefits section" of the D of E was proving to be very demanding. My colleagues and I had to calculate unemployment and DHSS entitlement, and we did so within vocal distance of outraged claimants demanding to know why their benefits had been stopped or reduced. The telephones constantly rang, and maintaining one's concentration was a struggle. The engineer was right — we were all zombies.

A few months later, I had occasion to go upstairs, to the employment section. The contrast was incredible, the staff were under no pressure at all. They each had their own little cubicle, were out of sight of the public, and they even had time to talk to one another. It occurred to me that this was Heaven and downstairs was Hell. Could I get a transfer to "Heaven"? I spoke to my supervisor, then to my manager. He told me the benefit procedure would soon be changing, from a manual, to a computerised system, and in view of this, he could not let an experienced officer transfer. I persisted; the transfer would not have to be immediate, I was prepared to wait. A year later, I got my transfer.

Time

If only I had the time
My castles I'd make real
My art both bold and vigorous
Would tell all that I feel

My novels full of morals learned
Would bare life to its mystic core
Expose its pettiness and trivialities
And mock its manifold bore

My verse, pithy and clear
Would spark and stimulate
Imagination of ordinary people
Who live and love and hate

But when I have the time
My Muse will not play ball
I think, and think, and think again
But nothing comes at all

Thirty-Five

I am now aware that the breakdown of my marriage occurred during momentous world events: such as the Cuban Missile Crisis, when Kennedy and Khrushchev just managed to avoid nuclear war; and then a year later, the assassination of John F Kennedy on the 22nd November 1963. I am ashamed to admit, at the time, these events hardly registered on my consciousness. I was so distraught by my own misery. Then, in 1968, *Robert* Kennedy was shot: first a president, then a senator. I was appalled — how could such a thing happen again?

During this period, the USA had almost half a million troops in Vietnam, the war was going badly and it was by no means certain which side was going to win — liberal western democracy or state tyranny. I thought so much depended on a strong America, but after this second assassination I felt the whole of the civilised world was crumbling. What could I do? I queued up outside the American embassy and signed the book of condolences.

Oddly enough, at the time, millions of hippies appeared to believe that human nature could be permanently improved by a youth movement based upon sex, drugs and rock and roll. I suppose the marketing of the Pill in 1962 gave this idea licence, for it liberated both men and women from the fear of unwanted parenthood. And promiscuity could find some justification in the writings of Sigmund Freud and Dr Wilhelm Reich, who argued that most neuroses were caused by Judaeo-Christian sex repression.

But as the sexual revolution gained momentum, so did the Vietnamese War. It started in 1964 and continued until 1975. It was an appalling war, and the anxiety of having to fight in it no doubt drove many young people to "tune in, turn on, and drop out" and indeed the mantra of these young people to "make love not war" did have an appeal. We in England didn't have the same excuse, but the hippy movement inspired a determination to create a better world and many young people embraced it.

When the Beatles fell under the spell of an Indian Guru, Eastern philosophy became fashionable. One heard people say, with the gravitas of transcendental significance, such things as, "First there is a mountain, then there is no mountain — then there is." Or, "Silence is the sound of one hand clapping." I suppose that sort of nonsense seemed to make more sense when under the influence of drugs, but not even six pints of best bitter could do it for me.

The thought of going to San Francisco with flowers in my hair would have had a certain appeal, especially as it seemed to include free sex, but of course, it was too far away. Closer to home was the Isle of Wight Festival, but caftan and beads were not for me. I felt too old for such abandonment. I did read *Zen and the Art of Motor Bike Maintenance*, but I failed there too — I just didn't get it.

The Swinging Sixties was not all froth and nonsense, however, if you were talented and in the right place, probably either London or Liverpool, there were many opportunities. The fashion industry blossomed: clothes, hair, music, photography — all became transformed by the creative endeavours of an artistic youth. It was a renaissance made possible by the expansion of university places.

As for *my* life, not even a fresh start in the civil service could solve all my problems. I still felt inadequate, insecure and lonely. When I was a teenager, meeting the fair sex was easier; there were dance halls. But in the meantime, the scene had changed, couples no longer touched and the loudness of the music made conversation impossible. I found I could not adjust to the new swinging scene.

Thirty-Six

In January 1969 I joined a club called NA (Neurotics Anonymous). Once a week we met above a pub in Marylebone, and it was there that Jack, a blind man, would listen to our hang-ups and bring psychological insight. Jack spoke with great authority and quoted many psychiatrists. It was great fun; I could get drunk and listen to people as inadequate as myself. During this period, I wrote two poems:

The Loser

He sat forlorn and rather sad
A little drunk and a little mad

I've seen him stand up to the local lout
Getting badly knocked about

On going to the local races
He loses his shirt and also his braces

He's a broken man who always tried
He never won and he never cried

The Game of Life

I have fought in the game of life
I fought hard to win, but I lost
The fighting has brought me much strife
But I never counted the cost

That is, I never had done so before
I never had time for such thought
I suffered my pain and sought more
And laughed at the worst life brought

But now I am broken and old
My ambition I never shall see
I wanted the best life could hold
Instead life had best of me

It would seem my muse likes only a troubled soul.

Thirty-Seven

I suppose it was sometime in 1970 that I joined a group called "Stag" (Second Time Around Group). It was a club for divorcees. They were all professional people, and I always drank too much. I'm surprised they tolerated me; I would go to parties with *two* bottles of wine. It was after one such debauch that I wrote the following short story.

The Bridge

It was a cold night — or rather morning — in March, and having spent another regrettable evening smoking and drinking too much, I was walking home, attempting to clear my head. But the clearer my head became, the more desolate I felt, and on reaching the middle of a bridge crossing the Thames I stopped midway and stared at the river. All those lights on either side, beacons of expectations and disappointments. What a farce my life had become! I leant over the parapet and stared into the murky depths below.

"Well, why not? I've had enough!"

I clambered rather awkwardly onto the parapet and then stood up, the cold wind smarted my face and I felt detached and exhilarated. But at that very moment of resolution, a loud, harsh cough distracted me. I turned my head and saw a very slovenly figure approaching. A man with unkempt hair and beard, wearing dirty, ill-fitting clothes — a tramp!

As he passed, he looked at me and said, "You'll find the water cold at this hour." And that was *all* he said, he then continued walking on without so much as a glance back. Indignation consumed me; I was furious. How dare that walking dust-heap not care whether I live or die! Why, our situations might more logically be reversed. I leapt off the parapet and ran after the wretched fellow.

"Hey, just a moment, I should like a word with you." He didn't stop or even turn his head.

"Well, what can I do for you?"

"I want to ask you something."

"Well, go ahead, I'm listening."

"I want to know, what makes *your* life worth living?"

"Curiosity," he replied.

"Curiosity!" I echoed. "What have *you* to be curious about?"

"Oh, what's around the next corner? Who I'll meet at the coffee stall? Where I'll sleep tonight? But right now, I should like to know why a fine gent like you should be wanting to do away with himself?"

I didn't imagine he would understand, but it all came out. I explained how weary I was of the same routine, that my life had become as predictable as a well-played record — a disc of a nonentity screaming against a background of mediocrity.

"Well," said the tramp after a while, "sounds like you won't be missed. Is there anyone, or anything, that you'll miss?"

I thought for a moment, "As I don't believe there is anything afterwards, I shall not be able to miss anyone or anything, shall I? You see, I have concluded that we are merely the machinery of nature, a nature that is trying to make another, better machine, and this process will continue forever — an eternal striving for perfection. Well, this little machine of mine is declaring itself redundant."

I thought the tramp wasn't going to reply — couldn't.

"I see. First you complain that you can't find a worthwhile place in life and then you decide life is a waste of time anyway. Isn't that what's called sour grapes?"

A clever old boy, this one. I didn't know what to say.

"Ah, here's the Ritz!" The tramp nodded his head towards an all-night coffee stall.

"I reckon as how you owe me a cup of coffee, for having saved your life."

"Saved my life!" I exclaimed.

"Well, you're still alive, aren't you? And when you buy me this coffee — and a pie, I'll give you the benefit of my philosophy."

What he told me has completely changed my life. I no longer want to jump off a bridge — I should just like the price of a coffee and a pie.

Thirty-Eight

The Inter-Varsity Club is, or was, a social group for university graduates. The club met once a week, and the activities included play readings, folk songs, a philosophy group, and discussions. It sounded wonderful, and I was encouraged by a friend to seek membership. I did so, but never having been to university, I was turned down.

My friend said not to worry — he had arranged everything; all I had to do was turn up at a certain time, on a certain date. He refused to explain further, and I wondered what strings he had pulled. On the appointed day, I found he had lodged an appeal on my behalf, and I had to convince a committee of my acceptability. My friend must have realised I would never have had the confidence to turn up, had I known of the appeal beforehand.

I enjoyed the IVC, especially the philosophy group. I was even persuaded to speak at Speakers' Corner in Hyde Park, and lost my voice in the process! Some of the more interesting books I was reading at that time (spring of 1970) included *A History of Western Philosophy* by Bertrand Russell.

Thirty-Nine

It was November 1970. I had recently moved into a bed-sit in Richmond-upon-Thames and this morning had set off for work as usual. That is, I went to Richmond Underground station, which is a terminus, and as others were getting off, I got on. The carriage quickly filled up and then a dozen or so youths got on. "That's him," someone shouted. Then angry words were uttered, followed by loud thumps — I realised somebody was getting a hiding.

After several seconds I was beginning to wonder when the attack would cease, but nobody seemed to be taking any notice. The loud thumps continued; it was none of my business. Perhaps the victim deserved what he was getting, anyway, I was at the other end of the carriage — surely somebody nearer would protest or intervene.

I could stand it no longer; whatever this person might have done I doubt if he deserved much more. I stood up and made my way down the carriage, "Stop! He's had enough." Suddenly the gang turned on me and I received some kicks and punches as they hurriedly left.

Now there were three remarkable things about this incident. One, the leader of the gang was the last to leave and he actually wanted to shake my hand. Two, nobody else either intervened or uttered any protest. Three, when I walked back to my seat, all eyes were averted. Those who had a book or a newspaper pretended to read, others looked at their feet — it was all so unreal and the silence was uncanny. I sat down bemused and disgusted. I felt I had more in common with the gang than with these people.

A few days later I saw the leader of the gang with some of his friends; they were on the other side of Richmond High Street. I was recognised, and thankfully ignored.

Forty

1971 was a better year for me. In April I completed a performing arts course at Richmond College and played a minor part in Noel Coward's *Still Life*, which, in spite of not having Rachmaninoff's Second Piano Concerto playing in the background, was reasonably successful. I also did a soliloquy from Shakespeare and devised a little scene in mime. It was all great fun.

In September I started a course at the City Literary Institute in Holborn. It was called "Fresh Horizons" and was a foundation course for mature students thinking of going on to university. My fellow students were very good company and most went on to a teacher training college. I had been full of self-doubt: would I be good enough, how would I survive without a regular income and indeed, did I really want to become a teacher? Before the decision had to be made, I received a substantial pay increase; it had been long overdue for civil service salaries had been kept low for some years.

***

In January 1972, I passed my driving test and a couple of months later bought a second-hand car — a white Triumph Herald with hooded chrome headlamps — a beauty. In April,

I started a part-time job as a petrol pump attendant. I was left in sole charge, and when the petrol and diesel were delivered, I had to climb on top of the tanker and measure the before and after capacity with a dipstick.

In July I went on holiday and visited Swanage, Charlestown, Mevagissey and Weston-Super-Mare. The long drive back home was quite tiring, and as I pulled up outside my residence the gear stick came away in my hand. How lucky was that! I hate to think what would have happened had it occurred earlier.

On returning to my garage, I learned that another part-time worker had been robbed of her till.

***

On visiting my parents, I found my father was dismayed to find a number of empty, or nearly empty, paint cans in the basement. Apparently, two men had delivered them and had then demanded £30 from my mother. "Jack needs them urgently for a job he's doing and we were promised cash on delivery," said one of the men. But my mother had been deceived, and my father was furious. After some deliberation, my father could only think that the two men might have come from the gambling joint down the road, that having been unlucky at cards they had made good their losses by conning my mother.

My father left the house determined to sort out whoever was responsible. I was alarmed. I had been unaware of the gambling joint until this morning and I wondered what trouble my father might find there. He was still quite fit but no longer a young man and he might be outnumbered. I made a quick decision, knowing that my father kept his tools under the stairs; I took out a slate hammer and concealed it under my coat. On following my father, I saw him enter the door beside the laundry and go up the stairs. It was several minutes before he reappeared, but by then he was satisfied that no one there was guilty. I would only have used the hammer in extreme circumstances: to prevent the use of a weapon, or my father getting a kicking.

***

I took the afternoon off (Christmas shopping time) to visit my parents and my brother David. I arrived with sherry and mince pies, but although I had given prior notice, only my mother was at home. David was shopping, and my father was in the "British Queen".

My mother wanted no sherry as she was drinking whiskey, nor did she want any mince pies, but then she went on to tell me that her gold locket and chain had "disappeared" from its case. She also said she was thinking of buying Dad a watch for Christmas, as he had sold his old one to David for beer money. She then went on to catalogue Dad's vices. I felt entirely at a loss to resolve these issues and I left for the "British Queen", where I found my father playing cards with his cronies.

The public bar of the local pub was my father's normal habitat; the recreation was cribbage, dominoes or darts. The conversation, sport or betting. One's standing in such company was measured by a capacity for drink and a liberal wallet. I remembered one such afternoon when, within half an hour, four pints were lined up for us to drink, sent over by my father's friends. As I was not much of a lunchtime drinker, I decided, on this occasion, to leave.

From time to time I would feel a sense of failure in not being able to relate to my parents in any meaningful way. Was I inadequate because they were? My father drinks because he is socially inept and only feels comfortable with his drinking companions, and my mother leads a reclusive, friendless existence, because my father hasn't allowed her enough freedom to improve her life. Sometimes, I felt an urge to drink to oblivion, but when I did, I awoke with a hangover and self-loathing.

Driving back to Richmond I got a speeding summons!

Forty-One

Over the years, from time to time, I have put my thoughts and anxieties on paper — mainly to keep sane. Most of those notes and diaries were later destroyed. I was ashamed of them — they were badly written, neurotic, self-centred and agonisingly soul searching — perhaps the same might be said of this book! However, I did keep some of the less embarrassing extracts and I thought it appropriate to include them here. They are not dated. They are just scraps salvaged from an embarrassing catalogue.

***

If you can be light-hearted, or even light-headed,
     Without losing all sense of balance
     If you can think hard, without losing all sense of fun;
     If you can criticise stringently, without becoming cold-blooded,
     Then you are a man, my son.
     My apologies to Rudyard Kipling.

***

Socrates believed it was the soul that distinguished man from the beast and that it is the duty of man to act in accordance with reason. Man has a responsibility to man — as well as God.

***

My four stages of man:
    Childhood — living life spontaneously
    Adolescence — the proud ego
    Young manhood — a growing self-awareness, and a need of identity
    Maturity — the desire for wisdom

***

If our feelings, desires and passions were never aroused, we would be incapable of love or anger; moreover, we would be morally paralysed and impassive to the grossest injustice. We communicate by feelings: a man taking hold of a woman's hand conveys more than a thousand words; love is more evident in the doing than the telling.

***

In *Trousered Apes,* a book by Professor Duncan Williams, "he sees the role of literature and the arts, not merely as a mirror passively reflecting whatever passes for contemporary social and cultural values, but as a powerful force which helps shape the way people seek to live and behave. He believes that literature should reflect an "ideal world" in order to inspire man with a vision of high possibilities. To deny man an ideal, to emphasise his primitiveness, to ignite his baser passions and depict him as a trousered ape, is not only a form of literary, artistic and philosophical dishonesty. It is a sin against life itself and a crime against humanity".

(I copied the above from the book jacket of *Trousered Apes* — by Professor Duncan Williams)

***

To talk and discuss, but not a dry intellectual discussion, rather a personal exchange of ideas about one's hopes, aspirations, sympathies and fears. Conversation at work is almost wholly utilitarian, expressing only routine facts and information. I hear no imaginative ideas; neither do I detect any subtle feelings.

***

I like Plato's parable, that we were once hermaphrodite — having the reproductive organs of both sexes — but we showed so much energy and enterprise, that the gods feared we would also become gods — so they divided us into male and female. We now spend so much energy seeking our other half, that we no longer are a threat to the gods.

***

Socrates believed that no one *knowingly* does wrong, that if they do, they had not properly grasped that it *was* wrong. I think J B Priestley illustrates this brilliantly in his play *An Inspector Calls*.

***

I'm beginning to think that Nietzsche was right when he said the morality of the herd is a slave morality — and that to overcome nihilism we need a Superman. God is dead, and we worship superficial media heroes, and then peep about, to find ourselves dishonourable graves.

***

A play on the radio argued that God needs the Devil, for without him good behaviour would be imperceptible; in the same way as an etching would be imperceptible, if all was black, or all white.

***

Sartre says, "Man is his own future." Is this true? I don't think so. We are not nearly as free as Sartre implies, we are in constant dialogue with our social environment, and our freedom depends on that dialogue. Simone de Beauvoir was right when she pointed out that, if women did indeed have the freedom of choice, why would they choose an inferior role to that of men? In fact, they chose nothing of the kind; their choices are limited by their traditional roles within a male-dominated society. Sartre should have read some sociology.

***

I sometimes believe we are like wicks, each tapping into a common source of fuel. I feel that life is interconnected, that life is evolving, that it is meaningful, or perhaps "seeking" meaning. We see the world, not as it is, but through the lenses of our perceptions and preferences. We need one another to see the world as it really is.

***

Do we control our thoughts and feelings, or do they control us? I sometimes believe that, for the most part, they control us. That they behave like playful fairies or mischievous imps. Some appeal to the mind, such as science and politics, others to the emotions.

We may not see these sprites, we may not be unaware of them, but subconsciously, like a siren's seductive call, they try to seduce us. Join me, one says, but I hesitate, where will you lead me? up a blind alley? through a jungle? or to a beautiful garden? Is the sprite merely playful, or is it a treacherous imp?

Or is this fanciful nonsense?

***

If I have understood correctly, P. D. Ouspensky, in his book *A Search for the Miraculous*, is saying, we have two "selves": a social self, that accepts the world as it is; and an essential self that must be trained to examine the world objectively. He maintains that a pre-occupation with "self" and materialism blinds us to that which is truly important. A quest for "enlightenment," on the other hand, entails seeing things as they are, seeing people and the world in the round, warts and all, but with compassion and understanding. Ouspensky says, because life appears to be full of pain and irresolvable contradictions, we erect "buffers" in order to make it more agreeable. "Buffers" enable us to love our pets, but ignore factory farming; to praise the Lord, while passing the ammunition; to be shocked by deaths at home, but indifferent to a million deaths abroad. "Buffers" give us an agreeable feeling that all will be well, that no contradictions exist; that each of us can sleep in peace, knowing we are right. "Conscience", on the other hand, is to experience a sense of responsibility for the conceits and injustices of the world.

***

The Wet Planet

"Tell me more about the wet planet, Daddy," the little girl said. "Last time you told me that intelligent life had developed a capitalist system which they could not control — that it became a society based upon greed and exploitation."

"Ah, yes," said the old man, "the wet planet. Well, as I told you, after some thousands of years' intelligent life discovered science and technology, which, had it been used in a rational and cooperative manner, could have promoted peace and goodwill. Instead, those people used their technology to develop weapons, and weapons led to war and violence.

149

"Had the intelligent people used their media and technology to pursue common, universal goals, they might have succeeded in bringing about a Utopia — they instead used their knowledge to gain power and wealth. Everything became a means to individual ends, conflicts arose and people struggled against one another. The resultant catastrophe became inevitable.

"Could we have done more to help, Daddy?" the little girl asked.

The old man reflected. "We did more than was allowed. We showed them the error of their ways and even warned them of the consequences should they not change, but alas, they were a flawed species: sentimental when they should have been rational, and rational when they should have been wise. Our advice became enshrined in superstition: partially digested ideas became sacred texts of iron authority, which enslaved rather than freed their intellect. Perhaps we should never have interfered."

***

Although I wrote the above many years ago, it seems even more relevant today. We seem to have imprisoned ourselves in a growth-for-profit-consumer-loving economy that is unsustainable. But it has proved so beneficial that few of us seem either willing or able to change direction. I sometimes feel we are like lemmings walking towards a cliff.

***

My philosophy course proposed the idea that human thought seems to be divided into two main trends. One, dating from Plato, suggests that humankind can determine the future by rationality. The other, dating from Heraclitus, holds that life is constantly in flux and that one can only adapt to ever-changing circumstances. Put simply, I suppose this is idealism versus pragmatism. But of course, humankind makes progress by zigzagging between the two.

Forty-Two

"There're Polish!" My friend Andrew nodded his head towards two girls at the next table, they were sitting with two men. Andrew, Polish by birth, joined in their conversation. The girls were quite attractive, but the one that especially caught my eye was called Barbara. She was wearing a shaggy, sheepskin coat and I thought she looked quite trendy. However, we had arrived just before closing time. We left, going our separate ways.

The following day Kasia, the other girl, stopped a man in the street to ask for directions and was invited to a party. I had also been invited to this party, for the person she stopped was another friend of mine, Sanghi. At the party I recognised Kasia and asked for Barbara's phone number, and after I had phoned Barbara the next day, she agreed to meet me at a pub at Notting Hill Gate.

In the pub, Barbara said that in her youth she had been a "lunatic". Now, I had dated some pretty strange girls, one or two of which would have suited that description, but this was the first one to admit it. After I had stopped laughing, Barbara explained that in Polish, "lunatic" meant sleepwalker. However, apart from this humorous misunderstanding, the evening was very boring. Barbara's

English vocabulary was very limited and I resolved never to see her again.

On the 14th December 1972, I was to learn that my wife had changed her name by deed poll, had two children and was living with a man. She petitioned for a divorce. I didn't object, I was happy for her. A week later, on a cold, miserable day, I was walking down an almost deserted Richmond High Street when, who should I see approaching from the other direction, Barbara! We had a coffee in the L'Auberge café.

After a few more meetings I took Barbara to my bed-sit and she spent the night with me. The following morning, we descended the stairs and found my Chinese landlady lying in wait for us, and she made it quite clear that she disapproved of our behaviour and I was told to start looking for alternative accommodation.

Barbara and I found a tiny bed-sit in Earl's Court. Our ground floor room looked out upon a tiny yard flanked by four high walls, and the sky was seen as though through a chimney. It was winter, it was bitterly cold, and the electric light, electric fire and a small Belling cooker, caused the meter to gobble up money like a voracious fruit machine.

This far from idyllic situation became worse when a young couple moved into the bed-sit next to ours. They persisted in playing their music at full volume and, as the party wall included a window, the sound penetrated remorselessly. I asked for the music to be turned down, but it never stayed down for long. When Barbara mentioned our situation to a Polish artist she knew, he offered to rent us a flat that had just become vacant in his house in Maida Vale.

The artist, Marek Zulanski was a tall, well-built man and he had the strong manly features of a Greek god. His silver hair added to his distinction, and although sixty-five years of age, he was very fit. I was to learn later that he had climbed mountains, and indeed, his brother had died that way.

After a brief introduction, Marek showed me a hemp rope and asked whether I would be able to climb it. I looked up. The rope dangled from one of the steel girders supporting the roof of his studio. Wanting to show off, I went up quickly, using only my hands. When I came down, Marek went up — and stood on top of the girder. "Come up," he invited. Going up a second time was harder, and I just managed to join him on top of the girder.

Our new accommodation was a nicely furnished studio flat. We shared a bathroom and kitchen with Marek, but had our own balcony and the use of a small garden. We were delighted with our new abode, but a month after moving in I found that Marek had asked Barbara to wash and iron his shirts, because we were "not quite paying a Maida Vale rent" — I felt inadequate, humiliated and resentful.

In order to work off some frustration I decided to join a weightlifting club in Kilburn High Road. I set off on a damp, dark evening and was halfway there when the heavens opened up. The rain fell in torrents, blurring out everything, but I pushed on blindly. Suddenly my knees buckled and I was up to my waist in water.

I was shocked, bewildered. What had happened! I then felt something in the water beside me, an enormous leaf — I was in a bloody lily pond! I had inadvertently stepped onto the surrounding coping, mistaking it for a step, and then — splash. Squatting there, with my umbrella above my head and up to my waist in water, I felt utterly ridiculous — what could I do, but laugh?

Marek lent me two books: *The Phenomenon of Man,* by Pierre Teilhard de Chardin, was written by a Catholic priest who held no doubts about the future of mankind or indeed of its destiny — we will all ascend to some "omega point" where we will be at one with our God. The other, *Chance and Necessity,* by Jacques Monet, was disconcertingly objective. It asserts that man is alone in the universe and that truth and inspiration is to be found, not in religion, but in moral responsibility based upon science. Mankind's destiny is solely dependent upon free choice, intellect and rationality.

The first book buoyed me up on currents of optimism, but with the second, I came down to earth with a wallop. Of the two, I thought Jacques Monet's account of the world was the more realistic. Moreover, the fact that he won the Nobel prize for biochemistry would certainly suggest that he knew what he was writing about.

It was now decision time: Barbara and I had been living together for one year — four months in Earls Court and eight in Maida Vale — but should we spend the rest of our lives together? The day before the wedding I had my doubts — not only was I unsure about our relationship. I was unsure about myself — what did I really want out of life?

I confessed my doubts to Barbara, and she cried and said she loved me. I was not wholly reassured, but I knew that without a marriage certificate Barbara would have to return to Poland. Might this be the real reason she wants to marry me, to remain in England? Oh, well, if it doesn't work out, we don't have to stay together.

We were married at Marylebone Registry Office on 16 March 1974. The wedding was a very quiet affair; Marek and his recent girlfriend, Maria, were witnesses, and in the evening my parents and my brother joined us in a small celebration. Incidentally, Barbara had introduced Maria to Marek just a few weeks before our marriage, and although Maria was 40 years his junior, they married in 1980 and had a son in 1983 — when Marek was seventy-five.

Forty-Three

The prospect of going to Poland was quite exciting. It was May 1974, and at the time Poland was on the other side of the Iron Curtain. It was Barbara's suggestion. She said it was time I met her family. Before going to Poland, I had to get permission from the Department of Employment, which was reassuring. I was a UK citizen, and my country was keeping a friendly eye on me.

On reaching Poland, I wondered what I would say or do if approached by the police or military. I thought I had better learn a phrase or two of Polish, just in case. I learnt, "Ja nie rozumiem ja jestem glupi Anglik," which is, "I am sorry, I do not understand, I am a stupid Englishman." I included the word "stupid," hoping to disarm any antagonism I might come across.

I need not have worried. Everybody I met was very friendly, but then there is always an exception! The exception in this case was a gorilla of a man with heavy stubble; he eyeballed me and approached in a most unfriendly manner, muttering something I did not understand.

Barbara overheard and said, "No, not German, English."

"Ah, English," he repeated. He then grabbed me in a bear hug and kissed me on both cheeks.

In Warsaw, I remarked on the huge layered skyscraper that reminded me of a wedding cake. Barbara was quick to tell me this "Palace of Culture" was the most unloved building in Poland. It was, she said, an unwanted gift from Russia and its only redeeming virtue was to provide one of the best views of Warsaw. Cynics said this was only because, from the top of the building, you couldn't see the building itself, whereas from any other part of the city, the building was a constant reminder of Russian dominance.

I suppose this ironic sense of humour enabled the Poles, at that time, to better cope with their lack of freedom. "How do you play Russian Roulette in Poland? — First, you form a group, then you tell anti-Russian jokes, then you try and guess who might be the traitor." Probably this sounds funnier in Polish, but I like this one: "Why do Polish police walk around in threes? Well, there must one who can read, and one who can write, and one more to keep an eye on those two intellectuals" Or, how about this, "What is two miles long and eats only cabbage? A Polish meat queue!"

Barbara's brother met us in Warsaw and took us to various places, including Auschwitz — a grim reminder of man's inhumanity to man. It was the scale of the killing that was so appalling — industrial genocide carried out with unremitting Germanic efficiency. I suspect, however, that terrible cruelty is endemic to the human race; all that is needed is "justification" and opportunity.

We then stayed in Gorlice, where I met Barbara's friends and family. After that I met some more of her friends in Zakopane, a skiing resort in the Tatra Mountains. The mountains provided a grueling terrain for walking, and after walking to a lake called the Eye of the Sea, I was quite tired. We also visited the lovely old city of Cracow.

It was an interesting holiday and I saw many places, but it felt more foreign than France or Spain; the language sounded more different and the words looked more different, and hardly anybody spoke English. The austerity of the country reminded me of Britain after the war, but I observed no deprivation among Barbara's friends — all of whom had good middle class jobs — in fact they could afford to be generous, too generous. I learned not to admire anything for fear of it being offered as a gift! My only complaint was not being able get a decent cup of tea.

Forty-Four

Working as a rat catcher for the local council might not appeal to everyone, but it was an indication of my state of mind at the time that it appealed to me. It was July 1975, and some months earlier my manager had told me I would never be promoted. It was not the first time I had applied for something new. Prior to that I had enquired about a job as a school caretaker, but when offered the job I had second thoughts and turned it down. Then, accommodation had been the lure, now it was the prospect of escaping an office environment. I was feeling frustrated and in need of a change.

Working in full view of both the public and my supervisor all day long allowed no privacy, no time for personal thought. Do not get me wrong — I enjoyed dealing with the public, the work was easy and I was good at it, but after a while it became a deadening routine.

I worked on the self-service section, which meant that people selected their own jobs from those on display. The jobs were for the unskilled, or skilled tradesmen, and all I had to do was phone the employer and arrange an interview.

One would regularly come across an unskilled man, or even a skilled one, who would argue he was far better off on benefits than in employment, and after he had reeled off the money paid for himself, his wife and three children, plus numerous other benefits, his case seemed unarguable. It was often the cost of accommodation that made working for a living unprofitable. We used several strategies to get these people back into employment, but with little lasting success.

If individuals did not attend regularly, we would bring them in with a letter threatening to cut their benefits. But claimants often got used to being unemployed, they would realise they could manage on benefits better than expected, and the luxury of free time became seductive. Alternatively, he, or exceptionally she, may have become demoralised — so it was important if possible, to get people back to work quickly or to suggest training or further education.

We also came across a number of tragic cases: a severely disfigured man would attend regularly to test his acceptability to another human being — we would reassure him and send him on his way; or a drug addict might claim he was unsuitable for work because of his addiction and he would pull up his sleeve to reveal scarred veins. Then there were transsexuals; most transsexuals, no doubt, manage to cross over with some degree of success, but we had one with a deep voice, and dark facial stubble, and the body of a navvy — she looked like a pantomime dame. One could feel nothing but pity for these people, but the tide of humanity was unremitting — how I longed for a little privacy.

Another of my tasks was to find employment for those on a Prison Hostel Scheme; this was an early release project for long-term prison offenders, those serving sentences of four years or more. When I first visited Wormwood Scrubs Prison, I was astonished to find that many of the prisoners had a dozen or more previous convictions for which they had never received a custodial sentence. There seemed a sense of inevitability about this — that a criminal, carried away on a tide of leniency, would inevitably progress to a more serious crime.

When interviewing someone who had committed an armed robbery or grievous bodily harm, I would sometimes wonder whether he would have committed such a crime if, after the first offence, he had been given a short stint of hard labour, followed by counselling to find out why the crime had been committed, and how, in future, the prisoner might avoid such criminality.

There is a lot to be said for that old adage: "a stitch in time saves nine". One might equally say: a stretch in time could save nine. Early intervention would save money, but of course, once the situation gets out of hand the cost of rehabilitation becomes prohibitive, and when the prisons become full, shorter sentences, or none at all, become inevitable.

On learning that long-term prisoners had the opportunity to study, I thought it very commendable. Then I learnt that one prisoner, who had been convicted of fraud, deception and embezzlement, was doing a course in business studies,

"He's going to be a right menace to society when he gets out," I exclaimed.

"It's the system," shrugged one of the staff in resignation.

I suppose most people commit crime, either consciously or unconsciously, as a rational/emotional way of coming to terms with their situation. Perhaps they find it necessary to bow to peer pressure. Perhaps they need to feed a "habit". Perhaps they feel it lends glamour or excitement to an otherwise impoverished life. Perhaps it is seen as the only way of obtaining a good life when all other doors seem closed. In fact, there are good reasons and bad excuses, but the establishment seems often not to know the difference. I was inspired to write another poem:

The Final Reckoning

"You are a thief," they said
But my "brief" knew better
He told the court to view my deed
In spirit and not in letter
"It shows great enterprise to steal
When you are desperate for a meal"

I later faced a murder charge
This time I had a "shrink"
"He's not to blame for this foul deed
He had no time to think"
Repression is the guilty foe
Created when denied the po

When I reached three score and ten
My end was drawing near
The priest, he was a kindly man
And did I see a tear?
"By repentance you begin
To win absolution for your sin"

And so it was I met my God
But he was not amused
"Free will, he said, is a holy gift
And should not be abused
Marx and Freud below you'll meet
And there the choice is cold or heat."

An appropriate way of dealing with crime will depend on what one believes are the causes of crime. If one believes the offender chose to be bad, rather than good (the moral argument), then punishment might well come to mind. If one thinks that crime is the consequence of poverty and unemployment (the sociological argument), then social reform would be recommended.

I would like to suggest one other possible cause — a poverty of mind and spirit (the spiritual argument). But if we require people to behave better, they have to see, feel and believe that it is in their own best interests. They should feel part of a community that guides and nourishes them. I am afraid that many aspects of our society only exploit, corrupt and deprave. Surely it should be the foremost aim of any society to produce good citizens.

I suppose a great many serious crimes are committed by people in thrall to drugs — which, of course, includes alcohol. Drugs confuse the mind, cause poverty and degrade the spirit. Unfortunately, drug-taking seems impossible to root out, and for many poor people around the world, the growing of cannabis, poppies, or the coca leaf, seems the only way they can survive. Why don't we recognise these two facts?

Could drugs be sold on world markets, like other commodities? Then the World Bank could buy them and take them out of circulation, or they could be legalised and controlled.

I thought the government might legalise the use of cannabis, but I was mistaken. They only decriminalised it. I thought tobacco companies should have been able to use the drug under license, they could then have ensured quality control, and the various strengths of cannabis could have been categorised — like tobacco. As it is, only the criminals, profit.

**

Incidentally, a nice man from the local council phoned me. He said I was too qualified for the job of rat catcher and that, should I be interested, better, more suitable jobs were available.

Forty-Five

June 1976

I have just finished reading *The Ascent of Man* by J. Bronowski. Barbara bought it for my birthday, knowing how much I enjoyed the TV series last year. It is about Man's long struggle to achieve his humanity.

13 August 1976

At last, a place of our very own. We have just bought a flat in Baron's Court. Yesterday we spent most of the day boxing up our possessions, and in the evening, we transferred all the boxes to our new flat. The stark, unadorned environment of our new abode was too much for Barbara and on looking around, she burst into tears. She missed our charming Maida Vale residence and thought we had bought unwisely.

I was happy with our new flat: we had two large rooms with interconnecting sliding doors, a partitioned off kitchen, three French windows and a lovely balcony. The bathroom was tiny, but that seemed a minor defect. But then we were both very tired, so I said, "Let's leave the boxes until tomorrow. What we need is a good meal and plenty of wine."

Next morning, in spite of a hangover, Barbara saw the flat in a more positive frame of mind.

23 February 1977

Today I learnt that I had passed the panel for the post of Executive Officer. I had been asked in September of 1975 whether I would like to be considered for promotion, and had perversely said no. I can now scarcely comprehend my past foolishness. I think at the time I wanted some reassurance that I would be suitable. I wanted to be told that I had earned promotion. I was smarting at the time from being told by my manager, some months before, that I would never be promoted. However, all's well that ends well.

8 Aug 1977

Since passing the panel I have been on two executive training courses, one in Liverpool, the other in Edinburgh. I enjoyed both immensely; the opportunity to learn, the competitive social atmosphere, and the excitement of exploring two unfamiliar cities, delighted me.

A small part of the Edinburgh course required two volunteers to argue an imaginary criminal case. I was one of two volunteers and we were each presented with the basic facts of a case that was so finely balanced with pros and cons, that either the "prosecution" or the "defence" could successfully argue it.

My opponent chose to prosecute, and I was downcast, for I had wanted to prosecute. I was even more downcast after he had presented his case, for he had done so with such vigour and clarity of thought that at first I could see no adequate defence. Then I remembered a book I had read some months previously, *Six Great Advocates* by Lord Birkett.

One of those forensic barristers had won his cases by making a strong *emotional* appeal. Could I do the same? I imagined I was selling vacuum cleaners and I looked each juror in the eyes. "Put *yourself* in this man's position . . . What *if* . . . How would *you* feel?" When the jurors started to nod their heads in agreement, I knew I was in with a chance.

The "jury," comprising the other course members, was out for nearly an hour (we found out afterwards that a very lively argument had taken place). Meanwhile, my opponent and I were on tenterhooks; this little piece of play-acting had assumed significance out of all proportion to its merits.

I was pacing up and down, smoking a cigarette, when the jury returned, and they brought in a verdict of "not guilty". My opponent was not a gracious loser — he went raving mad — I could not blame him. He had presented the more rational argument.

Forty-Six

1 January 1982

Barbara raised her glass and said, "Here's to another boring year!" When I questioned this, she asked what I had done for her and how many times had I taken her out. Is this a fair measure of a marriage? Why must a wife be so dependent on her husband for entertainment? Whatever happened to women's liberation and a sense of equality? I would never dream of blaming Barbara for a boring life, even though I might have greater cause. I suspect Barbara is envious of her sister Agnieszka, for she was taken by our neighbour Bruce to a New Year's Eve party last night — Barbara hates to miss out on anything.

Later in the day Agnieszka turned up and she and Barbara started talking in Polish — they were no doubt discussing the party. I was angry; Barbara accuses me of providing her with a boring life, yet she takes every opportunity to exclude me from hers. She refuses to teach me Polish and scoffs at any attempt I might make to speak the bloody language. We hardly spoke for the rest of the day, and I can't help feeling that this is not a very auspicious start to the New Year.

2 January 1982

In order to raise the cool social temperature, I bought a bottle of Scotch and some sparkling wine. In the evening, Bruce, Agnieszka, Barbara and I drank it all — and more besides.

3 January 1982

Hangovers were pretty common this morning.

7 January 1982

A radio programme about the Rastafarian movement: Rastafarians have a distinctive appearance. Their hair is worn in dreadlocks and they wear woollen hats of red, gold, and green; they eat no meat and they smoke marijuana. They consider themselves superior to the white race, so they keep to themselves and find inspiration in reggae music. They ascribe poor status to women — the duty of women is only to please men.

Rastafarians see themselves as exiles in "Babylon" (a place of sin) but come the millennium, they shall inherit the earth. Their spiritual leader is Haile Selassie of Ethiopia. The movement is symptomatic of a longing of Caribbean West Indians for a spiritual identity with Africa. They use the Bible in a selective self-justifying way — *well, I suppose they learned that from us whites.*

9 January 1982

I went to the IVC this evening and attended a lecture: "Infinity and Creation". The professor spent a lot of time stating how mysterious the concept of infinity was, but seemed to find it impossible to say anything meaningful, or to reach any kind of conclusion. In exasperation I asked whether he was talking about the infinity of space, or time, and whether this infinity had a start, but no end; or an ending, but no beginning; or with neither a beginning, nor an ending — for surely such definitions are important. The professor seemed a bit shaken by this and said he would agree with my conclusion, but not with my reasoning! I thought he was a silly old fool.

I returned home and watched a documentary called "A Small World" It described how "free trade zones" offer financial inducements to multinational companies by guaranteeing a passive work force — only women are employed and they work ten to twelve hours a day. As if that wasn't bad enough, the native crops are often destroyed to make way for cash crops. Thus food has to be imported. Consequently, the natives have to work to buy food, which, in the past, they might have grown for themselves. Thus, the workers become completely dependent upon their jobs. In the Philippines, such women receive no maternity benefits, and the poverty is such that babies sometimes get thrown away with the rubbish! Only those in power make money from the multi-nationals — the politicians become fat cats and the peasants become slaves. It is a globalisation of greed and misery.

10 January 1982
I spent much of the day vainly trying to de-freeze the water pipes on the flat roof. The pipes carry water from the tank and when frozen, we have no water at all.

12 January 1982
Yesterday, I tried in vain to buy an oil lamp. This morning, I bought a hurricane lamp in Kilburn High Road. This

afternoon, I placed the lamp next to the pipes on the flat roof and built a little shelter around them. This evening, running water!

15 January 1982

A TV programme stated that the profit from fraud is three times that of all other crimes, yet only a tiny number of police are assigned to deal with it — no wonder fraud increased by 50% last year!

A case that involves only tens of thousands of pounds, is considered too small to investigate; nor will the following be investigated:

Internal fraud

International fraud

Complex fraud

"Unintentional" fraud

One thousand extra inspectors have been assigned to catching "Social Security scroungers", but the number of inspectors dealing with other types of fraud has been reduced!

16 January 1982

This evening I watched Kenneth Griffith's documentary drama *The Most Valuable Englishman Ever*. It explained how Tom Paine — the 18th century writer and champion of freedom — became the most influential person in the American struggle for independence.

His work "Common Sense" explained why the American colonies should seek independence and how they would benefit by uniting under one flag. He took up arms on their behalf, and when all seemed lost, he wrote a rousing pamphlet that was read aloud to all the troops, and this so lifted their morale that the tide of defeat turned to victory.

Paine's book, *The Rights of Man*, so alarmed the English authorities that they sought to arrest him for libel and sedition — he escaped to France just in time, but was tried in his absence. The authorities paid for his name to be discredited and his book was burnt, together with his effigy, on the 5th of November. In Paris, he pleaded for the life of King Louis XVI, wishing to temper justice with mercy, but for this, Paine was imprisoned and he was lucky not to lose his head.

21 January 1982

Chris at work said, "Do you know the difference between your prisons and the prisons in my country?"

I said, "No."

He said, "In your country, a prisoner leaves the prison determined to have a good time before he returns. In my country (Nigeria) a prisoner leaves with the resolution, never, ever, to return, for the experience is too awful."

22 January 1982

This evening I saw a box of matches on the table, left, I believe, by Barbara's sister, Agnieszka. I noticed that they had been made in Russia. I left a note on the box, "You cannot expect a Russian match to strike." Well, it seemed amusing at the time.

25 January 1982

Barbara told me this evening that our marriage was over and that she was going to buy a bed-settee in order that we might sleep separately. Later, Agnieszka arrived and she and Barbara went out — probably to the pub.

The last time Barbara and her sister went to the local pub was when we were living in Maida Vale. On that occasion, Agnieszka accepted a drink from a man and then became alarmed on hearing that he kept a gun in his car and boasted of being a "hit man". Barbara, being more of a loving sister than a caring wife, brought this drunken man back to our flat, and after having explained Agnieszka's fears, she and her sister then went out again! I was furious and rather anxious, but I humoured the "hit man". The following evening, I visited the pub and spoke to some of the regulars. They told me the guy was a harmless fantasist and that his gun was an imitation.

The idea of Barbara wanting a divorce is quite ironic. Just before buying our flat I wrote to our solicitor requesting some advice on what our position would be, should we seek a divorce. Barbara was unaware of this letter and when she discovered the solicitor's reply, she went mad. Since then, our flat has manacled us together.

Barbara has many good qualities, but she so often gets stuck in her "parent". Perhaps she should be a teacher or a nurse, then this characteristic might be an asset, but I could well do without it. She is so critical — she criticises, me, my brother, my parents and my social class.

1 December 1982

James Lovelock developed his Gaia hypothesis in the early 1970s. He seems to be saying that the planet is, in some sense, a holistic, collective entity, and that it is, in some sense, alive. Lovelock noticed that the earth's atmosphere has remained remarkably constant, even though chemical processes ought to have made its composition change. His conclusion was that living organisms interact with the environment and keep it in a mutually beneficial equilibrium. Instead of life merely adapting to the environment, the two are linked in a self-regulating system. Lovelock described his idea as "a feedback of cybernetic systems, which seek an optimal physical, and chemical environment, for life on this planet".

3 December 1982

Barbara asked me to write a poem on a Christmas card that she was about to send to Poland. I wrote:

Christmas is a time of year, when all good friends
Both far and near
Should hope and pray the world will be
Nobler in its destiny

Writing that reminded me of a poem I had written about Christmas many years ago. The poem had been inspired by an incident I had observed. A mother was rowing with her drunken husband and was being harassed by her three young children. In exasperation, she exclaimed, "I wish Father Xmas had never existed!"

Of Christmas

Christmas is a time of cheer
Brought about by too much beer

We overeat and overspend
And call the most unlikely, "friend"

With gifts unwrapped and cards received
Are we really thus deceived?

Where's the fellowship of mankind?
Let us be good and let us be kind

Do away with ostentation
Then we may have true elation

Forty-Seven

9 January 1984

At the office, while interviewing a black man and his friend, I referred to a potential employer as, "the big white chief". On hearing this remark, one said to the other, "they are all the same" — implying "racists". I was deeply embarrassed; I blushed and stammered an apology.

Why on earth had I used such a term? It was an expression I hadn't heard or used for many, many years. It was the parlance Red Indians used in the Cowboy films I saw as a child. I think the term was later used ironically to describe any person in authority. This just goes to show how vulnerable we all are to accusations of being racist.

Years ago, society *was* racist, for the only blacks we ever saw, were in newsreels, where natives either performed war dances before members of our royal family, or were seen as servants in American movies. Consequently, many of my generation carry around some vocabulary we are ashamed of, and like a bad stroke in tennis, once "learnt", it is exceedingly difficult to eradicate.

Of course, when one meets blacks face-to-face, one realises they are no different from us whites — nor are the Germans, monsters, or the Japanese, inscrutable. We should each be judged by our behaviour, not by our vocabulary, for our speech is ingrained in our subconscious. One can only hope that with patience and goodwill, offensive terms will eventually be consigned to the rubbish bins of the past.

25 January 1984

Ann Leslie has written a series of articles in the Daily Mail: *Singapore — the city that conquered crime*. She describes Singapore as a fast-moving, highly commercial state, which has a multi-racial community living in dense housing conditions — all the ingredients that sociologists would predict leading to a high crime rate.

Yet Singapore has conquered its crime problems by a policy of stiff sentences. In the early 1970s, there was an alarming increase in armed robbery, so in 1974, the Armed Offences Act was introduced: if you fire a gun in the course of committing a crime, whether you actually kill anyone or not, the death penalty is mandatory; even the possession of a firearm, during a robbery, leads to life imprisonment. Rapists are caned and drug-pushers are hanged.

Almost the entire population now live in flats built by the Housing and Development Board. The family unit is used by the government as a "social policeman", and if just one member of a family acts in a criminal way, the whole family is evicted — it is reasoned that only by holding the entire family responsible will there be an incentive for each of them to behave well.

Anything that encourages families to break up is frowned upon: single people wanting to get away from their parents will not be offered accommodation by the government nor will single parent families. People living alone are considered one of the causes of crime and poverty.

Once, there was resentment among the tenants of ghettos that they were the deprived of society. In view of this it has become government policy to build blocks of flats that have a wide variety of accommodation, housing both the rich and the poor.

Anything which smacks of inefficiency, is out. Jury trials were considered inefficient because they often failed — out of muddle, or sentiment — to bring in a just verdict. So jury trials were abolished. It would also be inefficient to allow the population of an already overcrowded island to grow even bigger, so the government has decided to aim for zero population growth.

1 April 1984

Wojtek arrived today dressed as an Arab! His friend had just returned from Dubai and had bought him an Arab outfit as a present. Having a natural beard and dark complexion Wojtek looked a very genuine Arab. I then observed that our unusual visitor had not gone unnoticed by our neighbour Margaret, who lives in the balcony flat opposite. I then recalled us recently discussing our mutual intentions of selling our respective flats, and this gave me an idea. I asked Wojtek to follow me onto the balcony and to nod his head from time to time as I pointed out certain features. After this little performance I phoned Margaret and I told her that we had received a marvellous offer for our flat. The following conversation ensued:

"Did the Arab make the offer?

"Yes."

"But will he get a mortgage?"

"He wants to pay cash."

"Jeff, he wants to pay cash!"

I could hear Margaret relaying this information to Jeff, her partner, and she was getting increasingly excited.

"He has just shown me a case full of money."

"Jeff, he has shown Peter a case full of Money!"

"He would also like to buy some more flats nearby — for his wives."

Margaret shrieked. "Jeff! He wants to buy other flats nearby, for his wives!"

It was no good; I could no longer keep from laughing.

"April Fool!"

2 May 1984

This evening Barbara and I got a little drunk. We had a bottle of wine with our dinner and a few cans of beer afterwards. I tried to convince Barbara that a former headmaster of Rugby School, Thomas Arnold, was right when he said: first, moral principle; second, gentlemanly conduct; and third, academic ability. Barbara remained unconvinced and thought the reverse order more appropriate.

4 May 1984

This evening I watched *Tomorrow's World* and it reminded me of a discussion I had in the pub last week. On arriving at the pub, I found Nigel, his girlfriend Danielle, and two students, were talking at some length about the value of learning French — Danielle teaches it. I exclaimed that surely the learning of French was now a waste of time. It was a great attention-grabbing remark, and of course, they wanted to know why I felt that way.

I explained that recent experiments had identified the brain cells responsible for speech and that these had been transferred from one brain to another, making it possible to pick up a language in no time at all. I then said, "Of course, these experiments have only been carried out on rats" — they then realised I had been joking.

It had been quite a spontaneous joke; I was therefore fascinated to learn from today's *Tomorrow's World* that brain-cell transplants are indeed a reality and might one day lead to the cure of Parkinson's disease. But the cells would have to come from a fetus, for only those are capable of change and regeneration.

10 May 1984

I have been listening to one of a series of programmes about Christianity, called *Faith*. It appears that none of the Gospels are contemporary to Jesus Christ, they were all written a decade or more after he had died. Much of what was written was a restatement of pre-Christ rabbinical wisdom, which included allusions to a virgin birth, miracles and a resurrection. Most of the contradictory evidence to the Gospels was destroyed by Constantine when his Roman Empire embraced the faith.

The Christian faith has endured only because it has supported the needs and aspirations of both rulers and ruled.

14 May 1984

This evening I listened to a talk on the radio called *John Rauls — A Theory of Justice*. His basic premise is that all criteria should have universal acceptability and should be free of vested interest and prejudice. To achieve this neutral state of mind we should imagine we are outside society, that we have not yet been born, and that we have the job of deciding what we want society to be like.

Our decisions would have to be made knowing that we would have no idea of what tastes, talent or interests we might be born with, or whether we would be born into wealth or poverty. By this method, Rauls was striving for impartiality and he referred to this principle as "the veil of ignorance".

He believes society should maximise the life chances of all its citizens — the "principle of difference". He maintains that nobody has inalienable property rights, so if society can be improved by abolishing inherited wealth, then inherited wealth should be abolished. Nor should intelligence or talent have a right to the highest rewards, for our abilities stem from a common gene pool.

16 May 1984

Last night Barbara and I had a bottle of wine with our dinner and another bottle afterwards — we then drank some beer. I was trying to explain *John Rauls — A Theory of Justice*, but Barbara was unable to grasp even the first principle, and by the end of the evening, neither of us could understand anything.

Forty-Eight

1 July 1984

I learned today that two of my colleagues had passed their promotion panel. Sometimes I think I'm worthy of promotion, but at other times I consider myself lucky to be an Executive Officer. My memory is so treacherous — I can recall a name one moment, and the next I have forgotten it!

3 August 1984

David and I walked across Dartmoor from Ivybridge to Princetown. We had a wet start, but then the weather improved and we reached Princetown at 8.30 p.m. On arrival, we booked B&B at the "Plume and Feathers," had a hot meal, and then visited the other two pubs. Dartmoor consists of 365 square miles (you could visit one every day of the year).

4 August 1984

After what was described as a "Dartmoor breakfast," David and I walked to Yelverton. The countryside was more varied than yesterday's route, but we got caught in a heavy downpour. Fortunately, we found shelter under all that remained of an old miner's hut — the entrance — just one parallel slab of stone supported by two upright slabs, or a lintel supported by two columns.

Later in the day we heard a tremendous noise, and on crossing the brow of a hill we came across the Plymouth Leet — a metal conduit that conveys water for a considerable distance up hills and across dales. I believe it was constructed for the tin mining industry that was once common in the area.

We followed the Leet through thickets and barbed wire and eventually arrived at the village of Meavy, and from there we took the road to Yelverton and then a bus to Plymouth. At Plymouth we had a couple of Cornish pasties and a five-pint pub-crawl along the Barbican. The train back to Paddington left at 12.30 a.m. and arrived at 6.05 a.m. — it seemed to be full of hippies.

4 September 1984

Went to the local pub with my brother, David. We watched some "entertainer" whose act relied solely on vulgarity. I jotted down the following:

Obscenity, Crudity, Rudity.
Take your pick, you prick!
Culture is a vulture, to lift you out of shit,
You nit!
Choose elegance and grace
And join the human race
You're nothing but a disgrace
You twit!

Well, at least it made me feel a little less angry. Perhaps I'm just a prude.

5 September 1994

A TV documentary suggested that criminal justice in the USA is influenced by the dollar. Many criminals are not brought to justice because of reluctance on the part of the state, or the government, to instigate expensive criminal proceedings.

15 September 1984

David came to dinner and played a Rolling Stones' cassette. One track was especially beautiful — *As Tears Go By*.

19 September 1984

Today, Barbara and I flew to Malaga. Malaga has a fine promenade flanked by palm trees and gardens. It also has an attractive old quarter. After some refreshment we took the bus to Almunica, where we will be staying.

20 September 1984

We are staying at Las Gondolas, an apartment block that includes a swimming pool and tennis courts. We will self-cater during the day, but will eat out in the evenings.

This morning I climbed the craggy mass of rock alongside our apartment block. It is very steep and one has to find a zig-zag path to reach the top. On reaching the top my satisfaction was mixed with a queasy panic when I looked down on our apartment block — would I find a way down?

21 September 1984

This evening we climbed the narrow dusty streets of the San Miguel quarter and reached the Moorish castle at the top. The castle has seen many battles — the last was when the French bombarded it during the Peninsular War — and it is now used as a cemetery.

The tombs are stacked one on top of another and side-by-side, but my first view was of glass cases, each one containing a little shrine of remembrance, such as a photo, a crucifix, or a Madonna. So at first I thought these mementoes were *substitutes* for graves and coffins, and I was quite shocked when I saw the sarcophagi. The cemetery was rather derelict and some of the cases had been plundered.

We had dinner at Las Geranios, at the Plaza Evaristo Rivera. The bill was bigger than expected, and when I queried this a condescending waitress explained that the fish was priced by weight. After dinner, Barbara and I started to quarrel: there is a constant friction between us, usually just below the surface, and it makes its presence felt by implied criticism or sarcasm.

When we returned to our apartment, I discovered I had brought out the wrong key! On finding the night porter I waved my key at him "No funciona, por favor!"

22 September 1984

This morning Barbara wanted to know how I had managed to take the wrong key out last night. As I had already explained the circumstances of this tragedy of errors, I lost my temper, pushed her away and swore. After this we both tried to adopt our best behaviour. It is always the same lately: first a truce, then a cold war developing into open hostility.

We spent most of the afternoon beside the swimming pool — the ants here are only half the size of their British cousins, but they have twice the bite! I told Barbara that I had made a pact with them: they would die unless they behaved peaceably — they could touch, but not bite. After an hour, I told Barbara the pact had worked. She said it was my sweat that was the deterrent — she has no imagination.

Later in the day we took some photographs and had a good evening meal. It had been a good day — the truce held — and we made love.

23 September 1984

Another day of brilliant sunshine, I swam around the pool eighteen times. Barbara said it took me fifty minutes. In the evening we walked to El Santa, a high terrace on a peninsular called Penon del Santo — it is a prominent landmark as it displays a large illuminated cross. In the evening we had dinner in our apartment, roast chicken, tomatoes, bread and a litre of wine. I felt dreadfully tired afterwards, but Barbara wanted to argue about class and opportunity; she repeated her oft-made remark, that one can improve one's social standing by improving one's manners!

Barbara's sense of what is right and wrong is reminiscent of the etiquette that was current among the aspiring classes in the 1950s — such as *U and non-U* by Nancy Mitford. I actually read some of those books and I decided it was behaviour designed to reinforce class-consciousness and snobbery. Thankfully, most other people were of the same opinion, and such snobbery has now become redundant.

Barbara then started to complain about our boring life-style. When Barbara gets angry, I have visions of jackboots marching across Europe — could she have some German blood in her veins? The trouble is, she seeks constant entertainment and prestige, whereas I seek only self-fulfillment — and we are both frustrated. Sleep! O blissful sleep!

27 September 1984

This afternoon we sunbathed, and this evening we went to "Margaret Franz" for dinner — the white wine was served in a bucket of ice. Barbara said the food was very good, and we should return again soon. I agreed, and thought I might order paella for tomorrow, as it says on the menu that it is only cooked "by order" and must therefore be ordered in advance.

Barbara sneered and said this was nonsense. She said that one has to wait at the table for every meal and paella would be no different. She wouldn't leave the subject alone and went on to say how naïve I was, that I didn't know how to behave, that I had never been around enough and didn't know what was expected. On being given the bill, I asked the waiter how much notice should be given should I want paella. He said, "One day," and I asked Barbara for an apology.

30 September 1984

After dinner this evening Barbara ordered tequila. It was served with salt and lemon. This surprised and delighted Barbara, probably because she imagined that this gave her "sophistication". We later made love.

3 October 1984

Consternation — We had missed our nine a.m. taxi! I was angry; the night porter hadn't woken us in time, although I had generously tipped him, and now we would miss our flight! But the taxi was not late, we were early — the clocks had been brought forward an hour.

28 October 1984

The Case Against God presented by Gerald Priestland on Radio 4, recalled how some Jews in a concentration camp had put God on trial and found Him "guilty". However, after the verdict, and a brief silence, one of the Jews said, "And now let us pray." I thought at first this was sheer hypocrisy, but on reflection, I think I understand. I imagine Jews do not believe in a perfect God. Consequently, they feel free to criticise Him and to argue with Him directly, man to God. To me, this seems far healthier than slavishly praising God and beseeching him for mercy.

29 October 1984

I suppose each generation has been forced to consider the bigger picture. My generation has had to revise its ideas about blacks, gays, the disabled, and even women. And since the moon landings we have had to consider all the ramifications of a spaceship world — the fact that we all live in a vulnerable global village.

2 November 1984

This evening I finished a poem that I started on 21.10.84

Martyrdom

They came to jeer
From far and near
Not knowing their mistake

And all the time
Through pain and grime
He dragged along his stake

A demi-god mortal
Leaving ever more thoughtful
All those in his wake

7 November 1984

This evening I listened to the first of the Reith Lectures — *A Froth on Reality* by Professor John Searle, University of California. The subject was the mind-body problem — that is, how something as insubstantial as "mind" can relate to the "substance" of the brain. "Materialists" would have us believe that mind is no more than a superficial by-product of the brain, like the froth on the crest of a wave. But Prof. Searle argues that the dichotomy between mind and matter, is a mistaken one, that "mind" and "matter" are different *orders* of a singular phenomenon. He suggested "water" as an example. Water has both an atomic structure and the quality of liquidity. To consider one as the cause of the other, would be a mistake.

6 December 1984

Barbara *will* interfere when I'm brushing my hair, she thinks she knows better — she always knows better. I have many, many times put up with Barbara's petty interference and criticisms, only for the sake of peace and quiet, but last Sunday I exploded. Since then we have not exchanged one more word than was absolutely necessary. Not that this has made much difference; we seldom watch the same TV or listen to the same radio programmes. We share only our bitterness.

9 December 1984

How I envy the sensual extravert, as played by Anthony Quinn in *Zorba the Greek*. He might well have been talking to me when he tells the Alan Bates character that he has everything necessary to make a success of life, everything that is, "except a touch of madness, without this," Zorba said, "one cannot cut the rope and be free." I guess this is what Nietzsche meant when he said, "You need some chaos in your soul to give birth to a dancing star."

22 December 1984

I have an idea for a short story. I shall call it, "The Gods are Not Amused". It will be about the shortcomings of mankind as seen through the eyes of gods. The gods are not impressed by natural abilities such as good looks, physical strength, talent or intellect — for these are gifts from the gods themselves — nor do they demand perfection, for the gods are not perfect. Pious words and passive goodness have little value for the gods. What the gods *do* demand, is commitment — a commitment to a better future.

Forty-Nine

14 January 1985

Barbara infuriated me today. I had just returned from the gym, and she noticed I was wearing my polo shirt inside out. What a fuss! Barbara was not only critical, but offensively critical. In a rage I grabbed an earthenware vase from the kitchen table and hurled it at the French windows. Barbara then cried and disappeared into the bedroom, and I was left to pick up the pieces.

The vase had gone through two double-glazed panes and I had to chip out all the broken glass from putty that was concrete hard. The weather was literally freezing, and I nearly cried with the pain in my fingers. I then had to buy replacement glass and put it in.

This punishment was out of all proportion to any momentary satisfaction I might have achieved — punishment really does work. I resolved never to lose my temper again.

19 January 1985

During the last couple of days, I have been doing some personal stocktaking: I am nearly fifty years of age and have an empty shell of a marriage; it is virtually a mother son relationship, with Barbara the nagging mother and I the obedient, but resentful, child. Why do I stick it? But then again, where could I go? Where could Barbara go? We are bound together by our flat and mortgage; neither of us could survive separately, but together we have comfort and financial security. It is, however, a barren sort of life. I am enslaved by inertia and pacified by a fantasy expectation that one day the gods will smile on me.

10 February 1985

I have just finished a book by Jonathon Porritt, *Seeing Green*. It has completely blown my mind. It has made me realise that I have been, by temperament, an ecologist most of my life. I had thought that much of my thinking had been irrationally idealistic. Now, thanks to *Seeing Green*, I realise that far from being irrational, an ecological response to life is the only way we can survive.

12 February 1985

Perhaps in future the countries of the civilised world will seize the opportunity to create a world-order that will be truly democratic. Perhaps they will form a club that is so patently ethical and democratic, that other less fortunate countries will want to throw off the yoke of a dictatorship in order to join. Perhaps the West could create an ideology that would seduce the minds of the whole world, an ideology that would represent the common interests of *all* people, in all their varying circumstances — an ideology that would reveal our common interest.

17 February 1985

What is life all about? I suppose all the poets, artists and philosophers throughout the ages have tried to answer that question, but I must try and work it out for myself.

Are we here to discover justice? Well, yes, that is why we have a legal system. This system not only imposes punishment for transgressions, but it actually encourages people to behave better by providing equal opportunities and tolerance.

Are we here to reduce inequality? Well, yes, that is why we have politics and a welfare state.

Are we here to express ourselves? Well, yes, humankind has an unquenchable thirst for self-expression.

Are we here to satisfy our curiosity? Well, yes, the need to explore and investigate has always been a part of humankind's makeup.

Are we here to develop our consciousness? Well, yes, that is the purpose of art, literature and philosophy.

Are we here to be good? Well, yes, I suppose so. Isn't learning the difference between good and evil an intrinsic part in developing our consciousness, of deciding whether or not we are going to add some beneficial karma to the world?

Are we here to worship a God? Well, there certainly seems to be a worldwide *need* to do so. Some would say this need is based upon feelings of helplessness, and the hope of a better life hereafter. But others might say that religion brings strife as well as comfort to the world, whereas the welfare state brings only comfort. That might be so, but comfort of the body is not comfort of the soul.

Are we here to discover our soul? Well, I must confess, I can't think of a better reason, or a more controversial one. Whether the flowering of the human spirit constitutes a soul, is a matter of opinion. It is certainly evident that each one of us desires to be more than we are, but whether this striving has any transcendental significance, is also a matter of opinion. We will believe what we will, but what we believe, will surely be the making of us.

4 March 1986

This evening, I watched *Arena* on BBC 2. It was a documentary about the filmmaker Akira Kurosawa. The heroes of Kurosawa's films are constantly seeking enlightenment and self-knowledge. I was most impressed. I can't help thinking that good and evil are still relevant concepts: that every one of us contains a white knight and a black prince, each struggling for supremacy, and each will finally determine who we are.

23 March 1986

I spent most of the day finishing *Of Human Bondage* by Somerset Maugham.

14 April 1986

This evening I went to a fringe theatre at the Sun Inn, South Ealing. The play *Bazaar and Rummage* was written by Sue Townsend, the creator of *Adrian Mole*. It is a "comedy" about a group of inadequate and unlovable women — it should be called *Bizarre and Rubbish*.

22 April 1986

This evening Barbara went to a party at Urek's Yacht Club. I watched Truffaut's *La Peau Douce* on TV — super!

4 May 1986

I have played a lot of tennis these last few weeks. This afternoon I played my brother at Hartswood Lawn Tennis Club. This evening Barbara went to a Polish party.

11 May 1986

This afternoon I played David tennis in drizzling rain. Barbara went to visit Maria. This evening I read Karl Popper's *Unended Quest*.

14 November 1986

Today, Barbara and I took a day off work to see if we could buy a house. We were lucky, we have bought one, or to be more precise, we made an offer, and it has been accepted.

16 November 1986

This morning an incident occurred that has been bugging me all afternoon. David and I had just started to play tennis at Brook Green when approached by two women, one young, the other somewhat older, and they asked how long we intended to play. It was ten a.m. and we said we intended to play until eleven a.m., and from eleven a.m. my brother had booked the court in order to do some coaching. As the two women left, I regretted not having asked them if they would care to play mixed doubles.

16 December 1986

Life is an exploration into the unknown, an adventure to be experienced — not a mystery to be solved. But first, it is important to know oneself. Brodsky reminds us that self-consciousness is the "source" of our reality; it enables us not only to know ourselves, but also to "make" ourselves.

17 December 1986

I cannot understand how anyone can live in a world without meaning. For such a person, principles would be considered worthless, as indeed would all the finer emotions. It would surely lead to a life of opportunistic pleasure and exploitation, for nothing else would have any significance beyond its utilitarian value. Such a person would no doubt have psychopathic tendencies, leading to dominance, suicide or murder.

19 December 1986

Can one really believe the reductionism's theory: that all the brain functions can be reduced to neural activity — and nothing more? Can one really believe that all our behaviour is determined by such neural activity — and nothing more? If a primitive native found a radio, would he be right in thinking that the radio consisted of valves and resistors — and nothing more? Is music nothing more than sound waves? Is a painting nothing more than paint on canvas? Is a book nothing more than ink on paper?

Fifty

1 February 1987

We have sold our flat in Baron's Court and have moved into a little terraced house in Ealing.

4 March 1987

Barbara spotted a robin in the garden this morning and I immediately made up a poem.

Barbara said I should write it down, so I did:

The Robin

Robin, robin, on the wall
Do you have no food at all

Has my wife no food to spare
Not an apple, crust, or pear?

Barbara, Barbara feed this redbreast
Then the angels can their heads rest

9 March 1987

I was tempted to write that I am a born worrier, but no, that wouldn't quite be true. I have only become a worrier over the last twenty or thirty years. It has been a gradual process, based, no doubt, upon ignorance. I couldn't understand how this country was going to support itself economically when we appeared to be losing most of our industries. I couldn't understand how a world of limited natural resources could support an ever-growing number of people. Humankind seemed like a cancer that was rapidly spreading at the expense of all other life forms.

However, I now see that more jobs have been created by service industries and IT. I now know there is no shortage of food because the green revolution has enabled us to grow more food on less land. Furthermore, I now realise that technology is creating materials that are better than the ones they are replacing. But still I worry — am I only projecting my own insecurities on the world?

4 June 1987

Barbara returned from shopping just after I had vacuumed the whole house. She said I had not done a very good job, as I had missed a bit.

"Which bit?" I asked.

"The front room," she said.

"I have done the front room," I said.

"Then you didn't do under the window," she said.

"Why do you say that?" I asked.

"Because there's a dead fly beneath the window," she shouts.

"How do you know it hasn't just died?" I shout back.

"Because it was there first thing this morning!" she screams.

"How do you know it's the same fly?" I scream back.

"Because it's in exactly the same place," she shrieks.

June 1988

Moving to our present address has proved to be so very beneficial. We have made new friends and have each developed additional interests. I enjoy trying to write, and Barbara, tired of being a tennis widow, decided she would play tennis as well. I thought she would never learn, for she had no natural ability, but she persisted and now plays regularly. Barbara has also developed a passion for photography and competes at her local photographic society. We both love our computers, I, mainly for writing, and Barbara, for photography and emails.

***

26 March 1995

Next week I retire. My later years in the civil service have been good years; I worked for the Wages Inspectorate, then for the Appeals Tribunal and then for the Industrial Tribunals.

29 March 1995

Gillian Anderson, aka Dana Scully of X Files, is quoted as saying, "I believe we are here to learn, grow, and enrich our soul." I like that! I am not so sure about my "soul" — but I live in hope.

1 April 1995

My sixtieth birthday. I have retired from the civil service, and it is like being born again — but what will I do with all the extra time?

Fifty-One

How I used to hate the long, boring Sundays of my youth — an eternity of time with only the radio for company — for like most working class homes, my home was without books, gramophone records, or meaningful conversation — — boredom was the norm. I used to wonder why people wanted to live forever when they did not know what to do with themselves on a wet Sunday afternoon.

Nowadays, there is so much to do, to think about, and to experience, and when I recall those long, boring Sundays and compare them to the not quite long enough days of the present, I realise how very fortunate I am to have discovered the joy of reading. I am not a great reader, but for me, even a little learning is rewarding.

I feel sorry for those children who can only think of destructive things to do. I also feel sorry for those who have to teach such children. It must be enormously difficult to make education seem relevant to some of the feral children roaming our streets. If only one could instil in them the excitement, the wonder and the joy of learning. One doesn't have to be intelligent to enjoy learning. I am surely proof of that, but I am convinced that an enjoyment of learning is natural — if presented in the right way.

Would philosophy be a stimulant to learning? In Greek, philosophy means "love of wisdom". Plato (428 – 354 BC) said, "Philosophy begins in wonder," Socrates (470 – 399 BC) said, "To your own self be true." Incidentally, I find an echo of this in Jesus: "What shall it profit a man if he shall gain the whole world, and lose his own soul?" But what does being true to oneself mean? — Debate.

But what is wisdom and why did philosophy develop in ancient Greece? One could say that wisdom is to know the truth about what really matters in life. La Rouchefoucauld said, "Wisdom is to the soul what health is to the body." One possible explanation as to why philosophy developed in ancient Greece is that its geographical position allowed it to trade with other civilisations, and the wealth thus created, coupled with the stimulus of other cultures, allowed free men, the time and opportunity to think about life.

Plato's Academy and Aristotle's Lyceum encouraged the development of Politics, Ethics, Biology and Poetics, and such schools spread learning all over the Greek world. An example, surely, of how diverse civilisations can, when they learn from one another, benefit one another — perhaps a point worth making to the children of multi-cultural Britain.

In the ancient world philosophy stimulated thought and sought answers, but the spread of Christianity brought about intolerance and persecution. In 525, Justinian closed down all the philosophy schools and thus the Dark Ages began. Fortunately, ancient philosophy was preserved by the Muslim world, and this knowledge was brought back to Europe after the Crusades.

I am not entirely against religion, for although it has hindered progress and has been responsible for dreadful crimes, it has also inspired great art, good deeds and hope, but religion needs to be constrained within the bounds of rationality.

Perhaps a potted history of sociology could also be taught in secondary schools. This could explain how our lives are influenced by the constant struggle between the past and the present, the powerful and the powerless, the ignorant and the informed. Human rights — what are they? Are they sufficient? Human responsibilities — what are they? Why do some people ignore them? I would suggest that these subjects could come under the heading, "life studies", and they should be non-academic: that is, no exams, only debates. Of course, more demanding studies could be provided for those that want them.

I would also like to see children given a *feeling* for nature. I believe the Buddhists have the right idea; nature should be venerated. Perhaps Buddhists could visit our schools. Every time I see a sapling with its bough wantonly torn off, I feel a tinge of sadness. Sadness, not for the tree, I'm not that loony, but sadness for the attitude that wants to destroy rather than nurture. I do not want to sound too sentimental about this. We need to kill animals and plants, but it is our attitude to such killing that is important.

When I was a child, I attended a party given by Air Raid Wardens. My father must have bought a raffle ticket, for I received the 1st prize — a microscope. I was too young and stupid to appreciate the microscope at the time, but I did experiment a little. I remember viewing a droplet of water that I had taken from the kitchen drain in my garden. On focusing the microscope, I leapt back in alarm. However, those busy bacteria no longer fill me with fear. In fact, I am grateful to them, for without them my drain would become blocked. Only by understanding the purpose of nature will we appreciate it.

I believe all nature has a rightful place in the world; all right, sometimes something can be in the wrong place at the wrong time or, like locusts, develop at the expense of other life forms, but in the bigger picture, perhaps even biological explosions have their uses — they certainly don't seem to have any long-lasting consequences, for they collapse as soon as they consume their source of food. It is apparent that only humankind can multiply to the expense of all other life forms and get away with it. Well, so far!

***

I have read that the first form of life was blue-green algae and that this mutated into bacteria and protozoa. The bacteria led to the development of all animal life and the protozoa to the development of all plant life. Thus, we are related, not only to the birds and the bees, but also to the flowers and woodlands. So here we all are, fauna and flora, all trying to "make a living", and at the same time fulfilling a niche in nature's *strategy* — is there a *grand plan?* If there is, perhaps only we humans can fulfil it!

The Fall

Humpty Dumpty sat above all
Humpty Dumpty had a great fall

And all of his creatures
And all of his men
Are trying to put Him together again

Perhaps God is blind
And can only see the world He created
Through the eyes of man.

I don't want to get too sentimental about this. Much of nature is red in tooth and claw, but the struggle for survival has created a rich ecology of life forms, based, not on the strongest, or the most "ruthless," but on those most adaptive to their environment; like the ant and elephant, the plankton and the whale, the rose and the butterfly. These life forms are part of a web of mutual dependence and the loss of one may affect many.

Aldous Huxley, in his book *The Human Situation*, said, "If we want to be treated well by nature, we have to treat nature well. Surely, it is as a matter of plain fact that if we harm or destroy nature, nature will harm and destroy us." But we humans are a part of nature so isn't the same advice apt? If we want to be treated well by other human beings we have to treat them well, for if we try to harm or destroy them, they will try to harm and destroy us. We must learn to respect one another. I sometimes think we forget how interdependent we all are. We should thank the farmer for our daily bread and all the others who cater for our needs. A man's work is his precious bond with society — it is almost spiritual.

Fifty-Two

Over the years I have become more and more sceptical, I have seen many crazes come and go, most of which have sunk into the oblivion they no doubt deserved. Nevertheless, there are some things which, although I cannot entirely believe, neither do I entirely disbelieve — ESP, for example. Now there are two fundamental grounds for a belief in anything — empiricism and personal experience; the evidence for ESP based upon observation and experiment, seems far from conclusive, so I am left with personal experience. I must admit that my personal experience is not very substantial and it could probably be explained in a number of different ways, and yet? — Well, I will let you decide.

It was 1997 in the month of July. My wife's niece Magda had arrived from Poland, and my wife and I decided to take her to Cambridge. After visiting most of the universities, we saw a round Norman church, and on entering the church, I was captivated by the music. When I asked the woman working there if she knew what it was, she said she didn't, but that it was being played from a CD.

On our way home, Barbara asked if I would stop at an open-air market, as she wanted to buy some vegetables. At the market I bought three CDs, and when we arrived home,

Magda asked if she could play one. The very one she chose contained the music we had heard at the church.

Now, I am not a music lover; I scarcely ever buy CDs and I had never before bought any classical music. I did buy some pop records in the 50s and 60s, but that is beside the point. The point is, I did not know at the time what I was buying, but felt "an impulse" to buy. The music was Pachelbel's Canon. All right, I now know that this is a very popular piece, but at the time I was unfamiliar with it, so was Magda, and although I bought three CDs, I never did play the other two — such is my interest in music.

More recently I had trouble with my computer, each letter I entered replaced an existing one. I was infuriated and baffled — what was wrong? Then I "knew" that if I went to the local library, I would find a book that would help me. In the library, I went over to the section that had books for sale. There were three or four books on computers, and on picking one up, I opened it, turned a page, and saw what I wanted. It appeared that I had inadvertently gone into "overtyping mode" and that by pressing the "insert" key I would once again be in "insert mode".

Now make of these trivial examples what you will. I cannot remember any other instances, but then, years ago, my scepticism would have restrained me from acting on any such absurd impulses. It is only in recent years that I have become more in tune with my more sensitive and mystical side. In my youth I eradicated any sensitivity as being unmanly. When my first wife observed how my fingers wrapped around my thumb, she exclaimed, "How sweet!" I saw this as a criticism. Real men were not supposed to be "sweet".

Fifty-Three

January 2000

As I watch the tea, coffee and biscuits being dispensed from a squeaking trolley, I wonder if I will be heard above the clatter of the cups, saucers and small change.

A Search for a New Enlightenment

Having recently joined the Humanist Association I have been reading some of the back issues of your newsletter. September's issue states, in bold capitals, "THERE IS NO GOD. INTELLIGENCE & FRIENDSHIP CAN SOLVE OUR PROBLEMS." Now, personally, I think such a statement is liable to offend the majority of the world's population, and I fail to see how Humanism can promote peace and goodwill by being so dogmatically atheistic.

The Church of England has changed considerably over the years — you might even say it is a permissive church for there are very few strictures, and if it now encourages people to behave better and to lead happier lives, then why should we decry it? Roman Catholicism is far stricter, but its dogmatism enabled Poland to resist the harsh dominance of Communism — a resistance that might have contributed to the collapse of the Soviet Union, thus benefiting the free world. Would you tell a Polish patriot that his beliefs were wrong?

Beliefs survive because they fulfil some need. Socrates was wise because he realised he knew so little. He did not tell people their beliefs were wrong, but by question and answer, he encouraged them to examine the validity of their beliefs. Now the validity of a religious belief is impossible to establish, as it usually comes down to faith, a faith in religious values. But are the values of the believer and the non-believer so very different? I can think of no good reason why a good humanist and a good Christian should not sing to the same hymn sheet — metaphorically speaking. Don't we all want a better world? Don't we all want reasons to be hopeful?

But humanists will no doubt claim that religion is now redundant, that everything once provided by the Church is now provided elsewhere. That approval and condemnation comes, not from the Church, but from the State. That absolution comes, not from a priest, but from an agony aunt or social worker. What is more, human rights, which have never been provided by the Church, are now provided by the State.

However, although the Western world has never had it so good, one can detect a growing unease. We live in a rapidly changing world full of promises and problems; full of choices and decisions, full of opportunities and angst, and the consequential stress in our lives has led to drug-taking, alcoholism, pornography and crime. Many seem to have lost their way.

I believe spiritual truth is out there, awaiting discovery, just as scientific truth is out there, and like scientists we must prove the validity of the truths we possess and once established, build upon them. However, when we discover "truths" no longer reflect reality, then, like a good scientist, we must be prepared to look for truths that are more inclusive.

This word "inclusive" is all-important; we have developed from families to tribes, from tribes to kingdoms, from kingdoms to nations — and now we have to develop into citizens of the world. As we live by our beliefs it is essential to harmonise those beliefs, to seek common interests and a common destiny. However, this inclusiveness must also include the natural world; we must stop treating Mother Earth like a prostitute.

Some say the Bible gives us licence to rape the environment. For in the first chapter of Genesis we have God saying, "let man have domination over all living things", but the second chapter tells us, "the Lord God took man and put him in the Garden of Eden, to dress and keep it." Later we learn that "Adam gave names to all cattle, and to the fowl of the air." No, I do not think we can blame the Bible. Perhaps the sin of Adam and Eve was to forget that they were the *custodians* of the Garden.

Science informs us that Homo sapiens probably evolved less than 200,000 years ago, and our culture, and everything that makes us feel superior to the animals — to the *other* animals — evolved not much more than 10,000 years ago. Yet during the last two *hundred* years we have done more harm to the planet than the dinosaurs did in two *million* years. We are the first species able to determine, not only our own future, but also the future of the planet — it is an awesome responsibility.

But creating a better world will be profoundly difficult. I have read that the wars of the next millennium might be over water or oil — for various reasons, water, clean, unpolluted water, is becoming increasingly scarce in some parts of the world, and of course, water is a basic necessity for life — but then, so is oil. Oil is energy, cheap energy, but at the present rate of consumption it will run out within a hundred years.

Some scientists have even predicted a "greenhouse" global warming — a consequence of man-made atmospheric pollution. Should those scientists be right, the increase in global temperatures will expand the sea and melt the ice caps. The consequential flooding of islands and low coastal plains will make millions of people permanently homeless and the consequences for a poor, overcrowded country will be devastating — an increasing population with less, and less land to sustain it.

But what, you may ask, has all this to do with Humanism? What can humanists do in the face of such intractable problems? Well, I think all social solutions start with the individual. If we can improve our own life and values, then at least we will have done *something* to improve matters. But we must also believe that life has a higher meaning. Of course, every healthy person believes this, if only subconsciously: it is the reason an artist will sacrifice "all" for his art — Van Gogh and Gauguin, for example, and the reason why men and women will die for a cause.

But this higher meaning is, of course, a "transcendental" meaning — a meaning beyond self-interest — a belief that the future holds the key to the present. Perhaps some of you believe, as I believe, that our destinies will be shared, just as our past is shared, and that we are part of a continuum: that as we walk with the dead, future generations will walk with us, each contributing to a greater truth. Is it not exciting to believe in something greater than ourselves?

***

In retrospect, I am amazed at how long this speech was — and how passionate: I sound like an Old Testament prophet!

Although The Humanist Association did not endorse my views, some members of the audience were very complimentary: "a breath of fresh air" and "a vision for the 21st century". One man, on reading my speech in the newsletter, phoned me up to asked my permission to have it read out in his local church!

***

The above speech was written off the cuff. I do not claim to have any specialist knowledge — I just get carried away. I dare say, like everything else in this book, all I write says more about me than about the world I am writing about. But I would like to believe that life has transcendental significance, that there is a connection between past, present and future, far and near, the individual and the universal.

Collective Unconsciousness

Our thoughts come from... we know not where
Our feelings too, but don't despair
The past and present, far and near
Are close at hand, to rouse and cheer

For the limitless whole of eternal creation
Will be seeking expression through our inspiration
Leading us where, only time will tell
Will it be Heaven, or will it be Hell?

Fifty-Four

13th December 2001

Facing the Enemy: Everyman

The IRA bomb that destroyed Brighton's Grand Hotel in 1984, killed Sir Anthony Berry MP; and since then, his daughter, Jo Tuffnell, has been trying to make sense of what happened. The seventeen-year emotional journey led to her meeting her father's killer, Patrick Magee, who served fourteen years in jail for the crime. On camera, the two come face to face. "It's a cruel expression, but he was a *legitimate target*," says Magee. "Meeting you, though, I am reminded that he was also a human being, and that he was your father and your daughter's grandfather, and that's all lost." The extraordinary outcome of these meetings was that tension gave way to friendship.

This programme raised so many questions in my mind. Magee obtained a degree while studying in prison, but since his release, and partly as a consequence of the meetings with Jo Tuffnell, he has engaged in the peace process. He came across as a very sensitive, very civilised human being, but had I been Jo Tuffnell, I should have wanted him to have been more severely punished, or even executed.

But had he been more harshly treated, he would no doubt have been a very different type of person. What is more, if he and his fellow terrorists had been executed, they would not have been available to help to bring about a peace movement. On the other hand, had Magee been executed for his previous terrorist activities, Jo's father might not have been murdered.

Tuffnell deplores the death penalty; she was almost in tears when speaking of the execution of Timothy McVeigh who was responsible for a terrorist bombing in the USA. She believes that without dialogue, nothing can be learnt, or any agreement reached. In a way, I suppose she was proved right, for on the 26th March 2007 Rev. Ian Paisley and Gerry Adams met to discuss the future of Northern Ireland and announced that they would form a power-sharing government.

Fifty-Five

March 2003

Some years ago, a scruffy white tomcat turned up on our doorstep for the odd tit-bit, but as the days passed we noticed it was getting hungrier and its appearance more dishevelled. We were concerned; had this cat been made homeless or were we enticing it away from its proper home?

We decided not to encourage it further; we chased it away, shouting, "Go! Go!" However, when the cat's bright red collar disappeared, we were finally convinced, "GoGo" had been abandoned — and how can one resist the beseeching eyes of a cat that refuses to go?

GoGo became part of the family and for many years he thrived, but recently we noticed that he wasn't himself. He didn't eat and he drank too much. He even slept beside the neighbour's cat instead of fighting it! Then last Sunday he suddenly keeled over — as though blown off his feet by a strong wind, but there was no wind. He lay still for a few seconds and then slowly regained his feet. I went over to stroke him, but when I looked into his unseeing eyes I thought I saw death and I was deeply shocked. I made up my mind to take him to the vet the following day.

The following morning, I found him lying on his side with his four legs stretched out in rigor mortis. I wrapped him in a pillowcase, dug a hole in the garden, and buried him. I was inconsolable. I had to express my grief in words:

GoGo

You charmed us as a stray
And would not go away
Ignoring our rejection
You won our affection
And came to stay

Oh, what a handsome sight
With your fur of white!
You made us mad
You made us glad
You gave us delight

Whatever the weather
You chased fur and feather
But then you got old
And grew less bold
And fought, never

Now death has taken you
And I have buried you
But my grief
Brings no relief
And I know not what to do

Fifty-Six

Politics used to be so easy. If you were working class you voted Labour, and all other classes voted Conservative. Nowadays, everything is so complex; it is no wonder that many people fail to vote. I feel sure this is not apathy but confusion. How does one measure the various issues, and how should one "weight" each one? The biggest threat to Western culture used to be Communism; perhaps the biggest threat in future will be Islamic fundamentalism. I don't know much about the Muslim faith, but a lack of knowledge has never prevented me from expressing an opinion before, so here goes.

I have the impression the scientific and secular world is anathema to fundamental Islam; it is a belief system that discourages individual thought and favours ancient received revelation, this leads to a lifestyle that is modest, un-progressive and intolerant of difference. In contrast, Western life has provided individual liberty, freedom of expression, and a tolerance of all beliefs.

We criticise the extremists for their failure to adapt their values to the modern world; we say their women have no equality, and their culture seems austere and puritanical. But at one time our religious leaders were equally zealous, but over centuries they became more moderate — some might say, too moderate.

Although I should not want to live within an Islamic culture, I can well understand how some Muslims might see our culture through jaundiced eyes. In our secular, anything-goes culture, excess is everywhere: drink, drugs, pornography, gambling and debt — it must seem to many Muslims that we are, indeed, the tools of Satan. Let us hope that in the battle for hearts and minds we manage to reduce this gulf between us.

Fifty-Seven

I used to be proud to be British; it was quiet pride, so quiet that I was barely aware of it. Then gradually I began to realise that my perception of the world was changing, the reality no longer coincided with my former cherished beliefs. Any nostalgia for the past became juxtaposed against new evidence. I used to think that I lived in a culture that was second to none, a society in which the further you moved up, the more excellence you would find.

I suppose this must sound very quaint nowadays, but in a world where a gentleman's word was his bond, this concept seemed to have validity. I suppose my belief must come from school, books, films and radio. Of course, as I got older, the scales began to fall from my eyes, and it became increasingly apparent that my earlier concept was of a very narrow, privileged little world.

Nowadays our society is fairer and more enlightened: privilege has given way to equality of opportunity and prejudice has fallen to factual reappraisal. We now have gay rights, women's rights and racial equality. These changes came, not from the upper class, but from a newly educated middle class that demanded a fairer society.

In view of all these improvements, why did I use the past tense "I used to be proud to be British"? Well, as already indicated, disillusionment that the world was less noble than I had thought, but also disappointment with the here and now. One is increasingly aware of a growing underclass that all of us have to carry and suffer from. In my youth one never read about three generations of unemployed, or of children intimidating teachers, or of firefighters getting ambushed, or of hospital staff getting attacked.

The tragedy is, these issues should have been dealt with years ago. Now these problems are endemic. We have created a culture of dependency that will, in the long run, only lead to suffering. There are a lot of hungry, ambitious and intelligent people in the developing world, and they will soon be competing against us for the world's limited resources. By keeping the underclass in a state of dependency we are denying them the opportunity to compete.

It is a problem that will not go away, but then, most the prosperous middle classes are unscathed by such problems and some are too busy feathering their own nests: deception and fraud are increasing and greed is widespread. It would seem that greater opportunity without strong moral constraint and punishment can lead only to greater exploitation. This "survival of the fittest, anything goes" environment is allowing the rich and powerful to take over the world!

Oh, Peter, stop trying to understand the bloody world and go to bed.

Fifty-Eight

Armageddon? Let's start from basics: the experts are predicting global warming. They predict the sea will almost certainly rise and the weather will become more extreme. As a consequence, there will be widespread disruption, less land for agriculture, less land for people to live on and widespread strife. Inevitably, many people will die.

Can anything be done to prevent this scenario? The experts tell us the most we can do is to lessen the consequences by cutting back on our carbon emissions. The trouble is, few countries are prepared to do this because the economies of Western societies are based upon growth, and the idea of zero or negative growth is unthinkable. Then we have the developing countries such as China (1.3 billion people) and India (1.1 billion). They are just starting to develop their industries and they want the same standard of living as the West — they want good schools and hospitals and a better quality of life — and who can blame them?

I have just watched *The Age of Stupid* on TV. It would appear that one way of dealing with this problem is for the developed countries to reduce their carbon footprint until the developing countries draw level. We will then all walk hand in hand into the sunset as equals. I can't believe anyone is taking this seriously. Unless or until we can obtain unilateral agreement, we should use our coal to produce energy. We are in danger of weakening our economy at the very time when we need to be strong.

If the experts are right, it seems clear to me that worldwide catastrophe is inevitable, but those who survive will have learnt a grim and terrible lesson. But *who* will survive? I can only imagine those best placed to survive will be the super-rich, the powerful and the intelligent. In the meantime, countries must prepare as best they can by strengthening their economies and ensuring that their institutions are ready and able to adapt to changing circumstances. Only after the reality of the situation really hits home, might some worldwide agreements become possible.

But then again, the experts might be wrong!

Fifty-Nine

Writing this book has given me a better perspective: on my relationship with my family, my early marriage, my present marriage, and indeed, on myself — reasons enough to justify the effort. It is, however, my relationship with Barbara that has proved to be the most revealing. It has been a bumpy ride.

However, we are now much closer, and I think we are much better off together than we would have been alone. We have both learned to compromise — to accept one another's perceived shortcomings and to respect one another's virtues. Equally important, we have learned to appreciate how one another's strengths and weaknesses can dovetail to provide a stronger bond.

Perhaps the most telling difference between Barbara and me, has been in the mastery of the English language. Her facility with the language has taken years to develop, and she still lacks the subtlety and familiarity that one can expect from a native speaker. Consequently, the mesh of her understanding does not match the finer one of my own and I am never quite sure how much she fails to grasp.

On the other hand, Barbara is much more gregarious than I. She can strike up a conversation with anybody and remember not only their names, but also those of their partners and children. She spends hours on the phone speaking to her Polish friends and loves to socialise. I am more introverted, in a structured environment such as a club or classroom, I am not slow to make my presence felt, but in other situations I panic, my mind goes blank and I find difficulty in remembering names and faces.

Well, there you have it, I set out to tell the story of my life and I think I have succeeded — after a fashion. The writing has not been easy, I am obviously not a natural writer and I have had to write and re-write constantly, moreover, at times, the memories have been quite painful, but a dogged determination has seen me though.

I realise that much of what I have written must appear naive and immature, but I have attempted to reflect the views and attitudes that I have held at various stages of my life. Even now my views are constantly changing and I can only hope that a certain progressive maturity has become apparent.

Have I learned anything from life? Well, I feel privileged to be sharing a world with so many creative and talented people. When I look around I realise how much I owe to others, my house, computer, phone, radio, books, medical services — all come from people far more creative and intelligent than me — I sometime feel like a glow-worm among stars!

Have I any regrets? Of course, but then I have come to realise that without mistakes, there can be no personal growth, and I am probably as happy now as I have ever been.

27th November 2018

I found a publisher on my computer and sent them a letter. Encouraged by their reply, I took my book to their office on 11th December.

It was dark and raining when I got to the office. I walked through the door and saw the top of a woman's head behind a tall counter.

I handed her my parcel and she opened a cupboard, that contained a lot more manuscripts, and she added mine to the pile.

23rd January 2019

The publisher would like to publish my book!

This came as some consolation to me, as on 2nd January, I had slipped and broken my hip.

Last night I had a dream, I dreamt I was in heaven,

God was there, I seized my opportunity

"Dear God, could you please tell me the meaning of life?"

God smiled,

"Yes, I could, but it would take an eternity".